50 Canadian Ice Cream Recipes for Home

By: Kelly Johnson

Table of Contents

- Maple Walnut Ice Cream
- Nanaimo Bar Ice Cream
- Butter Tart Ice Cream
- Saskatoon Berry Ice Cream
- BeaverTail Ice Cream (inspired by the pastry)
- Blueberry Grunt Ice Cream
- Montreal Bagel Ice Cream
- Poutine Ice Cream (creative twist)
- Coffee Crisp Ice Cream
- Tiger Tail Ice Cream
- Peach Melba Ice Cream
- Caribou Tracks Ice Cream
- Prince Edward Island Potato Ice Cream
- Butter Tart Ice Cream
- Timbit Ice Cream (inspired by Tim Hortons' Timbits)
- Maple Bacon Ice Cream
- Smoked Salmon Ice Cream
- Nanaimo Bar Ice Cream
- Moose Tracks Ice Cream
- Saskatoon Berry Pie Ice Cream
- Blueberry Pancake Ice Cream
- Beavertail Pastry Ice Cream
- Poutine Ice Cream
- Butter Tart Ice Cream
- Coffee Crisp Ice Cream
- Tiger Tail Ice Cream
- Nanaimo Bar Ice Cream
- Maple Walnut Ice Cream
- Cherry Blossom Ice Cream
- Nanaimo Bar Ice Cream
- Saskatoon Berry Ice Cream
- Maple Butter Tart Ice Cream
- Butter Tart Ice Cream
- Blueberry Grunt Ice Cream
- Nova Scotia Blueberry Ice Cream

- Atlantic Lobster Ice Cream (a novelty flavor)
- Maritime Donair Ice Cream
- Nova Scotia Apple Crisp Ice Cream
- Quebec Maple Pudding Ice Cream
- PEI Potato Ice Cream
- Butter Tart Ice Cream
- Saskatoon Berry Ice Cream
- Canadian Bacon Ice Cream
- Butter Tart Ice Cream
- Blueberry Maple Ice Cream
- Tim Hortons Double Double Ice Cream
- Red Velvet Cake Ice Cream
- Maple Walnut Crunch Ice Cream
- Saskatoon Berry Swirl Ice Cream
- Maple Bacon Pecan Ice Cream

Maple Walnut Ice Cream

Ingredients:

- 1 cup pure maple syrup
- 2 cups heavy cream
- 1 cup whole milk
- 4 large egg yolks
- 1/2 cup chopped walnuts, toasted
- 1 teaspoon vanilla extract
- Pinch of salt

Instructions:

1. **Prepare the Base:**
   - In a medium saucepan, heat the maple syrup over medium heat until it starts to bubble. Reduce the heat to low and simmer for about 5 minutes, stirring occasionally.
2. **Make the Custard:**
   - In a separate bowl, whisk together the egg yolks and gradually whisk in about half of the hot maple syrup mixture. Pour the egg mixture back into the saucepan with the remaining maple syrup mixture.
3. **Cook the Custard:**
   - Cook the mixture over medium-low heat, stirring constantly, until the mixture thickens slightly and coats the back of a spoon (about 170°F on an instant-read thermometer). Do not let it boil.
4. **Cool the Mixture:**
   - Remove the custard from heat and stir in the heavy cream, whole milk, vanilla extract, and salt. Let the mixture cool to room temperature, then cover and refrigerate for at least 4 hours or overnight until completely chilled.
5. **Churn the Ice Cream:**
   - Churn the chilled mixture in an ice cream maker according to the manufacturer's instructions until it reaches a soft-serve consistency.
6. **Add Walnuts:**
   - During the last minute of churning, add the chopped toasted walnuts and let them mix evenly into the ice cream.
7. **Freeze:**
   - Transfer the ice cream to an airtight container and freeze for at least 4 hours or until firm before serving.

8. **Serve:**
    - Scoop the Maple Walnut Ice Cream into bowls or cones and enjoy the delicious Canadian-inspired flavor!

This recipe yields creamy, maple-flavored ice cream with a delightful crunch from the toasted walnuts, perfect for enjoying on a sunny day or as a sweet treat after a meal.

Nanaimo Bar Ice Cream

Ingredients:

- 1 cup heavy cream
- 1 cup whole milk
- 1/2 cup granulated sugar
- 4 large egg yolks
- 1/4 cup cocoa powder
- 1/2 cup sweetened shredded coconut
- 1/2 cup chopped walnuts or pecans
- 1 teaspoon vanilla extract
- 1/4 cup semisweet chocolate chips, melted (for swirling)

Instructions:

1. **Prepare the Custard Base:**
   - In a medium saucepan, heat the heavy cream, whole milk, and sugar over medium heat, stirring occasionally, until the mixture begins to steam. Do not let it boil.
2. **Whisk Egg Yolks:**
   - In a separate bowl, whisk the egg yolks until smooth. Gradually pour about half of the hot cream mixture into the egg yolks, whisking constantly to temper the eggs.
3. **Combine and Cook:**
   - Pour the tempered egg mixture back into the saucepan with the remaining cream mixture. Cook over medium heat, stirring constantly with a wooden spoon or spatula, until the mixture thickens and coats the back of the spoon (about 170°F on an instant-read thermometer).
4. **Add Cocoa Powder and Flavorings:**
   - Remove from heat and whisk in the cocoa powder until fully incorporated. Stir in the vanilla extract. Let the mixture cool to room temperature.
5. **Prepare Nanaimo Bar Mix-Ins:**
   - In a small bowl, combine the shredded coconut and chopped walnuts or pecans.
6. **Churn the Ice Cream:**
   - Once the custard base has cooled, churn it in an ice cream maker according to the manufacturer's instructions until it reaches a soft-serve consistency.
7. **Layer and Swirl:**

        - In the last minute of churning, add the coconut and nut mixture to the ice cream and let it mix evenly. Drizzle in the melted chocolate and allow it to swirl into the ice cream for a marbled effect.
8. **Freeze:**
        - Transfer the ice cream to an airtight container, smoothing the top. Cover and freeze for at least 4 hours or until firm before serving.
9. **Serve:**
        - Scoop the Nanaimo Bar Ice Cream into bowls or cones and enjoy the rich, chocolatey flavors reminiscent of the beloved Nanaimo bar!

This recipe captures the essence of the Nanaimo bar in a refreshing frozen dessert, perfect for any occasion where you want to savor a Canadian favorite in ice cream form.

Butter Tart Ice Cream

Ingredients:

- 1 cup heavy cream
- 1 cup whole milk
- 1/2 cup packed brown sugar
- 4 large egg yolks
- 1/4 cup maple syrup
- 1 teaspoon vanilla extract
- 1/2 cup chopped pecans or walnuts
- 1/2 cup raisins (optional)

Instructions:

1. **Prepare the Custard Base:**
    - In a medium saucepan, combine the heavy cream, whole milk, and brown sugar. Heat over medium heat, stirring occasionally, until the mixture begins to steam. Do not let it boil.
2. **Whisk Egg Yolks:**
    - In a separate bowl, whisk the egg yolks until smooth. Gradually pour about half of the hot cream mixture into the egg yolks, whisking constantly to temper the eggs.
3. **Combine and Cook:**
    - Pour the tempered egg mixture back into the saucepan with the remaining cream mixture. Cook over medium heat, stirring constantly with a wooden spoon or spatula, until the mixture thickens and coats the back of the spoon (about 170°F on an instant-read thermometer).
4. **Add Maple Syrup and Vanilla:**
    - Remove from heat and stir in the maple syrup and vanilla extract. Let the mixture cool to room temperature.
5. **Prepare Butter Tart Mix-Ins:**
    - In a small bowl, combine the chopped pecans or walnuts and raisins (if using).
6. **Churn the Ice Cream:**
    - Once the custard base has cooled, churn it in an ice cream maker according to the manufacturer's instructions until it reaches a soft-serve consistency.
7. **Add Mix-Ins:**

- In the last minute of churning, add the nut and raisin mixture to the ice cream and let it mix evenly.
8. **Freeze:**
    - Transfer the ice cream to an airtight container, smoothing the top. Cover and freeze for at least 4 hours or until firm before serving.
9. **Serve:**
    - Scoop the Butter Tart Ice Cream into bowls or cones and enjoy the creamy, caramel-like flavors reminiscent of a traditional Canadian butter tart!

This recipe captures the essence of butter tart in a refreshing frozen dessert, perfect for enjoying on its own or as a delightful accompaniment to your favorite Canadian-inspired treats.

Saskatoon Berry Ice Cream

Ingredients:

- 2 cups Saskatoon berries (fresh or frozen)
- 1 cup heavy cream
- 1 cup whole milk
- 3/4 cup granulated sugar
- 4 large egg yolks
- 1 teaspoon vanilla extract

Instructions:

1. **Prepare Saskatoon Berry Puree:**
    - In a blender or food processor, blend the Saskatoon berries until smooth. Strain the puree through a fine-mesh sieve to remove seeds. You should have about 1 cup of Saskatoon berry puree.
2. **Prepare the Custard Base:**
    - In a medium saucepan, heat the heavy cream, whole milk, and sugar over medium heat, stirring occasionally, until the mixture begins to steam. Do not let it boil.
3. **Whisk Egg Yolks:**
    - In a separate bowl, whisk the egg yolks until smooth. Gradually pour about half of the hot cream mixture into the egg yolks, whisking constantly to temper the eggs.
4. **Combine and Cook:**
    - Pour the tempered egg mixture back into the saucepan with the remaining cream mixture. Cook over medium heat, stirring constantly with a wooden spoon or spatula, until the mixture thickens and coats the back of the spoon (about 170°F on an instant-read thermometer).
5. **Add Saskatoon Berry Puree and Vanilla:**
    - Remove from heat and stir in the Saskatoon berry puree and vanilla extract. Let the mixture cool to room temperature.
6. **Chill the Mixture:**
    - Cover the mixture and refrigerate for at least 4 hours or until completely chilled.
7. **Churn the Ice Cream:**
    - Once chilled, churn the mixture in an ice cream maker according to the manufacturer's instructions until it reaches a soft-serve consistency.
8. **Freeze:**

- Transfer the churned ice cream to an airtight container, smoothing the top. Cover and freeze for at least 4 hours or until firm before serving.
9. **Serve:**
    - Scoop the Saskatoon Berry Ice Cream into bowls or cones and enjoy the delicious, fruity flavors unique to Canadian Saskatoon berries!

This recipe captures the natural sweetness and nutty notes of Saskatoon berries in a creamy ice cream, perfect for enjoying as a refreshing summer dessert.

BeaverTail Ice Cream (inspired by the pastry)

Ingredients:

- 1 cup heavy cream
- 1 cup whole milk
- 1/2 cup granulated sugar
- 4 large egg yolks
- 1 teaspoon vanilla extract
- 1 teaspoon ground cinnamon
- 1/2 cup mini chocolate chips (optional)
- 1/2 cup crushed cinnamon sugar BeaverTail pastry pieces (recipe below)

Cinnamon Sugar BeaverTail Pastry Pieces:

- 1 sheet of puff pastry
- 2 tablespoons melted butter
- 1/4 cup granulated sugar
- 1 teaspoon ground cinnamon

Instructions:

1. **Prepare the Custard Base:**
    - In a medium saucepan, heat the heavy cream, whole milk, and granulated sugar over medium heat, stirring occasionally, until the mixture begins to steam. Do not let it boil.
2. **Whisk Egg Yolks:**
    - In a separate bowl, whisk the egg yolks until smooth. Gradually pour about half of the hot cream mixture into the egg yolks, whisking constantly to temper the eggs.
3. **Combine and Cook:**
    - Pour the tempered egg mixture back into the saucepan with the remaining cream mixture. Cook over medium heat, stirring constantly with a wooden spoon or spatula, until the mixture thickens and coats the back of the spoon (about 170°F on an instant-read thermometer).
4. **Add Vanilla and Cinnamon:**
    - Remove from heat and stir in the vanilla extract and ground cinnamon. Let the mixture cool to room temperature.
5. **Churn the Ice Cream:**

- Once cooled, churn the mixture in an ice cream maker according to the manufacturer's instructions until it reaches a soft-serve consistency.

6. **Prepare BeaverTail Pastry Pieces:**
   - Preheat the oven to 400°F (200°C). Line a baking sheet with parchment paper.
   - Roll out the puff pastry sheet and brush it evenly with melted butter.
   - In a small bowl, mix together the granulated sugar and ground cinnamon. Sprinkle the cinnamon sugar mixture evenly over the buttered puff pastry.
   - Roll up the puff pastry sheet tightly from one end to the other. Slice the rolled pastry into 1/2-inch pieces.
   - Place the pastry pieces on the prepared baking sheet and bake for 12-15 minutes or until golden brown and crispy. Let cool completely, then crush into small pieces.

7. **Add Mix-Ins:**
   - During the last minute of churning, add the crushed cinnamon sugar BeaverTail pastry pieces and mini chocolate chips (if using). Let them mix evenly into the ice cream.

8. **Freeze:**
   - Transfer the BeaverTail Ice Cream to an airtight container, smoothing the top. Cover and freeze for at least 4 hours or until firm before serving.

9. **Serve:**
   - Scoop the BeaverTail Ice Cream into bowls or cones and enjoy the delicious flavors reminiscent of the popular Canadian pastry!

This recipe combines the nostalgic flavors of cinnamon, sugar, and pastry into a creamy ice cream, making it a delightful homage to the beloved BeaverTail treat.

Blueberry Grunt Ice Cream

Ingredients:

- 2 cups fresh or frozen blueberries
- 1/2 cup granulated sugar
- 1 tablespoon lemon juice
- 1 cup heavy cream
- 1 cup whole milk
- 1/2 cup packed brown sugar
- 4 large egg yolks
- 1 teaspoon vanilla extract
- 1/2 teaspoon ground cinnamon

Instructions:

1. **Prepare Blueberry Compote:**
   - In a medium saucepan, combine the blueberries, granulated sugar, and lemon juice. Cook over medium heat, stirring occasionally, until the blueberries release their juices and the mixture thickens slightly (about 10-15 minutes). Remove from heat and let cool completely.
2. **Prepare the Custard Base:**
   - In a medium saucepan, heat the heavy cream, whole milk, and brown sugar over medium heat, stirring occasionally, until the mixture begins to steam. Do not let it boil.
3. **Whisk Egg Yolks:**
   - In a separate bowl, whisk the egg yolks until smooth. Gradually pour about half of the hot cream mixture into the egg yolks, whisking constantly to temper the eggs.
4. **Combine and Cook:**
   - Pour the tempered egg mixture back into the saucepan with the remaining cream mixture. Cook over medium heat, stirring constantly with a wooden spoon or spatula, until the mixture thickens and coats the back of the spoon (about 170°F on an instant-read thermometer).
5. **Add Vanilla and Cinnamon:**
   - Remove from heat and stir in the vanilla extract and ground cinnamon. Let the mixture cool to room temperature.
6. **Chill the Mixture:**
   - Cover the mixture and refrigerate for at least 4 hours or until completely chilled.

7. **Assemble the Ice Cream:**
    - Once chilled, churn the custard base in an ice cream maker according to the manufacturer's instructions until it reaches a soft-serve consistency.
8. **Swirl in Blueberry Compote:**
    - During the last minute of churning, add spoonfuls of the cooled blueberry compote to the ice cream and gently swirl it in for a marbled effect.
9. **Freeze:**
    - Transfer the churned Blueberry Grunt Ice Cream to an airtight container, smoothing the top. Cover and freeze for at least 4 hours or until firm before serving.
10. **Serve:**
    - Scoop the Blueberry Grunt Ice Cream into bowls or cones and enjoy the delightful combination of creamy ice cream with swirls of sweet blueberry compote!

This recipe captures the essence of a classic Blueberry Grunt dessert in a refreshing frozen form, perfect for enjoying as a summer treat or any time you crave the flavors of Canadian blueberries.

Montreal Bagel Ice Cream

Ingredients:

- 1 cup heavy cream
- 1 cup whole milk
- 1/2 cup granulated sugar
- 4 large egg yolks
- 1 teaspoon vanilla extract
- 1/2 cup chopped Montreal bagel pieces (recipe below)
- 1/4 cup maple syrup or honey (optional, for added sweetness and flavor)

Montreal Bagel Pieces:

- 1 Montreal-style bagel (sesame or poppy seed)
- 1 tablespoon unsalted butter, melted
- 1 tablespoon granulated sugar
- 1/2 teaspoon ground cinnamon

Instructions:

1. **Prepare Montreal Bagel Pieces:**
   - Preheat the oven to 350°F (175°C). Slice the Montreal bagel into small pieces.
   - In a bowl, toss the bagel pieces with melted butter, granulated sugar, and ground cinnamon until evenly coated.
   - Spread the coated bagel pieces on a baking sheet lined with parchment paper. Bake for 8-10 minutes, or until golden and crispy. Let cool completely.
2. **Prepare the Custard Base:**
   - In a medium saucepan, heat the heavy cream, whole milk, and granulated sugar over medium heat, stirring occasionally, until the mixture begins to steam. Do not let it boil.
3. **Whisk Egg Yolks:**
   - In a separate bowl, whisk the egg yolks until smooth. Gradually pour about half of the hot cream mixture into the egg yolks, whisking constantly to temper the eggs.
4. **Combine and Cook:**
   - Pour the tempered egg mixture back into the saucepan with the remaining cream mixture. Cook over medium heat, stirring constantly with a wooden

spoon or spatula, until the mixture thickens and coats the back of the spoon (about 170°F on an instant-read thermometer).
5. **Add Vanilla and Bagel Pieces:**
    - Remove from heat and stir in the vanilla extract. Let the mixture cool to room temperature.
    - Once cooled, stir in the chopped Montreal bagel pieces.
6. **Chill the Mixture:**
    - Cover the mixture and refrigerate for at least 4 hours or until completely chilled.
7. **Churn the Ice Cream:**
    - Once chilled, churn the custard base in an ice cream maker according to the manufacturer's instructions until it reaches a soft-serve consistency.
8. **Freeze:**
    - Transfer the churned Montreal Bagel Ice Cream to an airtight container, smoothing the top. Cover and freeze for at least 4 hours or until firm before serving.
9. **Serve:**
    - Scoop the Montreal Bagel Ice Cream into bowls or cones and enjoy the unique combination of creamy ice cream with crunchy, sweet bagel pieces reminiscent of Montreal's famous bagels!

This recipe brings together the flavors and textures of Montreal bagels in a fun and creative ice cream, perfect for indulging in a taste of Montreal's culinary heritage. Adjust sweetness and bagel crunchiness to suit your taste preferences!

Poutine Ice Cream (creative twist)

Ingredients:

- 1 cup heavy cream
- 1 cup whole milk
- 1/2 cup granulated sugar
- 4 large egg yolks
- 1 teaspoon vanilla extract
- 1 cup French fries, cooked and chopped into small pieces (recipe below)
- 1/2 cup cheese curds, chopped into small pieces
- 1/2 cup beef gravy (homemade or store-bought)

French Fries:

- 1 large potato, peeled and cut into thin fries
- Vegetable oil, for frying
- Salt, to taste

Instructions:

1. **Prepare French Fries:**
    - Heat vegetable oil in a deep fryer or large pot to 350°F (175°C).
    - Fry the potato fries in batches until golden brown and crispy, about 3-4 minutes per batch. Remove and drain on paper towels. Season with salt to taste. Let cool completely, then chop into small pieces.
2. **Prepare the Custard Base:**
    - In a medium saucepan, heat the heavy cream, whole milk, and granulated sugar over medium heat, stirring occasionally, until the mixture begins to steam. Do not let it boil.
3. **Whisk Egg Yolks:**
    - In a separate bowl, whisk the egg yolks until smooth. Gradually pour about half of the hot cream mixture into the egg yolks, whisking constantly to temper the eggs.
4. **Combine and Cook:**
    - Pour the tempered egg mixture back into the saucepan with the remaining cream mixture. Cook over medium heat, stirring constantly with a wooden spoon or spatula, until the mixture thickens and coats the back of the spoon (about 170°F on an instant-read thermometer).
5. **Add Vanilla and Mix-Ins:**

- Remove from heat and stir in the vanilla extract. Let the mixture cool to room temperature.
- Once cooled, stir in the chopped French fries and cheese curds until evenly distributed.

6. **Chill the Mixture:**
   - Cover the mixture and refrigerate for at least 4 hours or until completely chilled.
7. **Churn the Ice Cream:**
   - Once chilled, churn the custard base in an ice cream maker according to the manufacturer's instructions until it reaches a soft-serve consistency.
8. **Add Gravy Swirl:**
   - During the last minute of churning, drizzle the beef gravy into the ice cream and gently swirl it in for a savory touch.
9. **Freeze:**
   - Transfer the churned Poutine Ice Cream to an airtight container, smoothing the top. Cover and freeze for at least 4 hours or until firm before serving.
10. **Serve:**
    - Scoop the Poutine Ice Cream into bowls or cones and enjoy the unique blend of savory and sweet flavors reminiscent of Canada's iconic poutine dish!

This recipe offers a playful twist on traditional ice cream flavors, combining the unexpected elements of fries, cheese curds, and gravy into a creamy frozen treat. Adjust seasoning and ingredients to suit your taste preferences for a truly memorable dessert experience!

Coffee Crisp Ice Cream

Ingredients:

- 1 cup heavy cream
- 1 cup whole milk
- 1/2 cup granulated sugar
- 4 large egg yolks
- 1 teaspoon vanilla extract
- 1/2 cup coffee-flavored chocolate bars (such as Coffee Crisp), chopped into small pieces
- 1/4 cup brewed coffee or espresso, chilled

Instructions:

1. **Prepare the Custard Base:**
   - In a medium saucepan, heat the heavy cream, whole milk, and granulated sugar over medium heat, stirring occasionally, until the mixture begins to steam. Do not let it boil.
2. **Whisk Egg Yolks:**
   - In a separate bowl, whisk the egg yolks until smooth. Gradually pour about half of the hot cream mixture into the egg yolks, whisking constantly to temper the eggs.
3. **Combine and Cook:**
   - Pour the tempered egg mixture back into the saucepan with the remaining cream mixture. Cook over medium heat, stirring constantly with a wooden spoon or spatula, until the mixture thickens and coats the back of the spoon (about 170°F on an instant-read thermometer).
4. **Add Vanilla and Coffee:**
   - Remove from heat and stir in the vanilla extract and chilled brewed coffee or espresso. Let the mixture cool to room temperature.
5. **Chill the Mixture:**
   - Cover the mixture and refrigerate for at least 4 hours or until completely chilled.
6. **Churn the Ice Cream:**
   - Once chilled, churn the custard base in an ice cream maker according to the manufacturer's instructions until it reaches a soft-serve consistency.
7. **Add Coffee Crisp Pieces:**

- During the last minute of churning, add the chopped coffee-flavored chocolate bars (like Coffee Crisp) to the ice cream and let them mix evenly.

8. **Freeze:**
   - Transfer the churned Coffee Crisp Ice Cream to an airtight container, smoothing the top. Cover and freeze for at least 4 hours or until firm before serving.

9. **Serve:**
   - Scoop the Coffee Crisp Ice Cream into bowls or cones and enjoy the rich coffee flavor and crispy chocolate pieces reminiscent of the beloved Canadian chocolate bar!

This recipe captures the essence of Coffee Crisp in a creamy, frozen dessert form, perfect for coffee lovers and fans of the iconic Canadian treat. Adjust the amount of coffee flavor and chocolate pieces to suit your preference for a deliciously satisfying ice cream experience.

Tiger Tail Ice Cream

Ingredients:

- 1 cup heavy cream
- 1 cup whole milk
- 1/2 cup granulated sugar
- 4 large egg yolks
- 1 teaspoon vanilla extract
- Zest of 1 orange
- Orange food coloring (optional)
- 1/2 cup black licorice candy, chopped into small pieces

Instructions:

1. **Prepare the Custard Base:**
   - In a medium saucepan, heat the heavy cream, whole milk, and granulated sugar over medium heat, stirring occasionally, until the mixture begins to steam. Do not let it boil.
2. **Whisk Egg Yolks:**
   - In a separate bowl, whisk the egg yolks until smooth. Gradually pour about half of the hot cream mixture into the egg yolks, whisking constantly to temper the eggs.
3. **Combine and Cook:**
   - Pour the tempered egg mixture back into the saucepan with the remaining cream mixture. Cook over medium heat, stirring constantly with a wooden spoon or spatula, until the mixture thickens and coats the back of the spoon (about 170°F on an instant-read thermometer).
4. **Add Vanilla, Orange Zest, and Coloring:**
   - Remove from heat and stir in the vanilla extract and orange zest. Add orange food coloring if desired for a vibrant orange hue. Let the mixture cool to room temperature.
5. **Chill the Mixture:**
   - Cover the mixture and refrigerate for at least 4 hours or until completely chilled.
6. **Churn the Ice Cream:**
   - Once chilled, churn the custard base in an ice cream maker according to the manufacturer's instructions until it reaches a soft-serve consistency.
7. **Add Licorice Pieces:**

- During the last minute of churning, add the chopped black licorice candy to the ice cream and let it mix evenly.
8. **Freeze:**
    - Transfer the churned Tiger Tail Ice Cream to an airtight container, smoothing the top. Cover and freeze for at least 4 hours or until firm before serving.
9. **Serve:**
    - Scoop the Tiger Tail Ice Cream into bowls or cones and enjoy the unique combination of orange-flavored ice cream with ribbons of black licorice candy!

This recipe captures the distinctive flavors of Tiger Tail Ice Cream, popular in Canada for its refreshing citrus notes and hint of licorice sweetness. Adjust the intensity of orange zest and licorice candy according to your taste preferences for a delightful frozen treat.

Peach Melba Ice Cream

Ingredients:

- 2 cups ripe peaches, peeled, pitted, and chopped
- 1/4 cup granulated sugar
- 1 tablespoon lemon juice
- 1 cup heavy cream
- 1 cup whole milk
- 1/2 cup granulated sugar
- 4 large egg yolks
- 1 teaspoon vanilla extract
- 1/2 cup raspberry sauce (store-bought or homemade)

Instructions:

1. **Prepare the Peach Puree:**
    - In a blender or food processor, blend the chopped peaches, granulated sugar, and lemon juice until smooth. Strain through a fine-mesh sieve to remove any solids. You should have about 1 cup of peach puree.
2. **Prepare the Custard Base:**
    - In a medium saucepan, heat the heavy cream, whole milk, and granulated sugar over medium heat, stirring occasionally, until the mixture begins to steam. Do not let it boil.
3. **Whisk Egg Yolks:**
    - In a separate bowl, whisk the egg yolks until smooth. Gradually pour about half of the hot cream mixture into the egg yolks, whisking constantly to temper the eggs.
4. **Combine and Cook:**
    - Pour the tempered egg mixture back into the saucepan with the remaining cream mixture. Cook over medium heat, stirring constantly with a wooden spoon or spatula, until the mixture thickens and coats the back of the spoon (about 170°F on an instant-read thermometer).
5. **Add Vanilla and Peach Puree:**
    - Remove from heat and stir in the vanilla extract and peach puree. Let the mixture cool to room temperature.
6. **Chill the Mixture:**
    - Cover the mixture and refrigerate for at least 4 hours or until completely chilled.
7. **Churn the Ice Cream:**

- Once chilled, churn the custard base in an ice cream maker according to the manufacturer's instructions until it reaches a soft-serve consistency.
8. **Swirl in Raspberry Sauce:**
    - During the last minute of churning, add spoonfuls of raspberry sauce to the ice cream and gently swirl it in for a marbled effect.
9. **Freeze:**
    - Transfer the churned Peach Melba Ice Cream to an airtight container, smoothing the top. Cover and freeze for at least 4 hours or until firm before serving.
10. **Serve:**
    - Scoop the Peach Melba Ice Cream into bowls or cones and enjoy the creamy peach flavor with the tangy raspberry swirl, reminiscent of the classic Peach Melba dessert!

This recipe combines the refreshing taste of peaches with the tartness of raspberries in a creamy ice cream base, perfect for enjoying as a summer dessert or any time you crave a fruity and indulgent treat. Adjust sweetness and fruit ratios according to your taste preferences for a personalized Peach Melba experience.

Caribou Tracks Ice Cream

Ingredients:

- 1 cup heavy cream
- 1 cup whole milk
- 1/2 cup granulated sugar
- 4 large egg yolks
- 1 teaspoon vanilla extract
- 1/2 cup fudge sauce (store-bought or homemade)
- 1/2 cup mini peanut butter cups, chopped into small pieces

Instructions:

1. **Prepare the Custard Base:**
    - In a medium saucepan, heat the heavy cream, whole milk, and granulated sugar over medium heat, stirring occasionally, until the mixture begins to steam. Do not let it boil.
2. **Whisk Egg Yolks:**
    - In a separate bowl, whisk the egg yolks until smooth. Gradually pour about half of the hot cream mixture into the egg yolks, whisking constantly to temper the eggs.
3. **Combine and Cook:**
    - Pour the tempered egg mixture back into the saucepan with the remaining cream mixture. Cook over medium heat, stirring constantly with a wooden spoon or spatula, until the mixture thickens and coats the back of the spoon (about 170°F on an instant-read thermometer).
4. **Add Vanilla:**
    - Remove from heat and stir in the vanilla extract. Let the mixture cool to room temperature.
5. **Chill the Mixture:**
    - Cover the mixture and refrigerate for at least 4 hours or until completely chilled.
6. **Churn the Ice Cream:**
    - Once chilled, churn the custard base in an ice cream maker according to the manufacturer's instructions until it reaches a soft-serve consistency.
7. **Add Fudge Sauce and Peanut Butter Cups:**
    - During the last minute of churning, add the fudge sauce and chopped mini peanut butter cups to the ice cream and let them mix evenly.
8. **Freeze:**

- Transfer the churned Caribou Tracks Ice Cream to an airtight container, smoothing the top. Cover and freeze for at least 4 hours or until firm before serving.
9. **Serve:**
    - Scoop the Caribou Tracks Ice Cream into bowls or cones and enjoy the creamy vanilla base with swirls of fudge and delightful bites of mini peanut butter cups!

This recipe captures the essence of Caribou Tracks Ice Cream with its rich chocolate fudge swirls and mini peanut butter cups, making it a decadent and indulgent treat for ice cream lovers. Adjust the amount of fudge sauce and peanut butter cups according to your preference for a perfect balance of flavors and textures.

Prince Edward Island Potato Ice Cream

Ingredients:

- 1 cup heavy cream
- 1 cup whole milk
- 1/2 cup granulated sugar
- 4 large egg yolks
- 1 teaspoon vanilla extract
- 1 cup mashed Prince Edward Island potatoes, cooled (recipe below)
- Pinch of salt

Mashed Prince Edward Island Potatoes:

- 1 large Prince Edward Island potato, peeled and cubed
- Water, for boiling
- 2 tablespoons unsalted butter
- 2 tablespoons whole milk
- Salt, to taste

Instructions:

1. **Prepare Mashed Prince Edward Island Potatoes:**
   - In a medium saucepan, bring water to a boil. Add the cubed potato and cook until tender, about 15 minutes.
   - Drain the cooked potatoes and return them to the saucepan. Mash the potatoes with butter, milk, and salt until smooth. Let cool completely.
2. **Prepare the Custard Base:**
   - In a medium saucepan, heat the heavy cream, whole milk, and granulated sugar over medium heat, stirring occasionally, until the mixture begins to steam. Do not let it boil.
3. **Whisk Egg Yolks:**
   - In a separate bowl, whisk the egg yolks until smooth. Gradually pour about half of the hot cream mixture into the egg yolks, whisking constantly to temper the eggs.
4. **Combine and Cook:**
   - Pour the tempered egg mixture back into the saucepan with the remaining cream mixture. Cook over medium heat, stirring constantly with a wooden spoon or spatula, until the mixture thickens and coats the back of the spoon (about 170°F on an instant-read thermometer).

5. **Add Vanilla, Mashed Potatoes, and Salt:**
   - Remove from heat and stir in the vanilla extract, cooled mashed Prince Edward Island potatoes, and a pinch of salt. Mix until well combined and smooth. Let the mixture cool to room temperature.
6. **Chill the Mixture:**
   - Cover the mixture and refrigerate for at least 4 hours or until completely chilled.
7. **Churn the Ice Cream:**
   - Once chilled, churn the custard base in an ice cream maker according to the manufacturer's instructions until it reaches a soft-serve consistency.
8. **Freeze:**
   - Transfer the churned Prince Edward Island Potato Ice Cream to an airtight container, smoothing the top. Cover and freeze for at least 4 hours or until firm before serving.
9. **Serve:**
   - Scoop the Prince Edward Island Potato Ice Cream into bowls or cones and enjoy the unique combination of creamy ice cream with the subtle sweetness of mashed potatoes, showcasing the island's culinary heritage!

This recipe offers a creative twist on ice cream by incorporating Prince Edward Island's famous potatoes, creating a smooth and slightly savory dessert that's both intriguing and delicious. Adjust the sweetness and texture to your liking for a perfect treat that celebrates the flavors of PEI.

Butter Tart Ice Cream

Ingredients:

- 1 cup heavy cream
- 1 cup whole milk
- 1/2 cup granulated sugar
- 4 large egg yolks
- 1 teaspoon vanilla extract
- 1/2 cup chopped pecans or walnuts, toasted
- 1/2 cup butter tart filling (recipe below)

Butter Tart Filling:

- 1/2 cup packed brown sugar
- 1/4 cup unsalted butter, melted
- 1/4 cup maple syrup or corn syrup
- 1 large egg, beaten
- 1 teaspoon vanilla extract
- Pinch of salt

Instructions:

1. **Prepare Butter Tart Filling:**
    - In a bowl, combine the brown sugar, melted butter, maple syrup or corn syrup, beaten egg, vanilla extract, and salt. Mix until smooth and well combined.
2. **Cook the Filling:**
    - Transfer the mixture to a small saucepan and cook over medium heat, stirring constantly, until it thickens slightly (about 5-7 minutes). Remove from heat and let cool completely.
3. **Prepare the Custard Base:**
    - In a medium saucepan, heat the heavy cream, whole milk, and granulated sugar over medium heat, stirring occasionally, until the mixture begins to steam. Do not let it boil.
4. **Whisk Egg Yolks:**
    - In a separate bowl, whisk the egg yolks until smooth. Gradually pour about half of the hot cream mixture into the egg yolks, whisking constantly to temper the eggs.
5. **Combine and Cook:**

- Pour the tempered egg mixture back into the saucepan with the remaining cream mixture. Cook over medium heat, stirring constantly with a wooden spoon or spatula, until the mixture thickens and coats the back of the spoon (about 170°F on an instant-read thermometer).

6. **Add Vanilla and Butter Tart Filling:**
    - Remove from heat and stir in the vanilla extract. Let the mixture cool to room temperature.
    - Once cooled, stir in the cooled butter tart filling and chopped toasted nuts until evenly distributed.
7. **Chill the Mixture:**
    - Cover the mixture and refrigerate for at least 4 hours or until completely chilled.
8. **Churn the Ice Cream:**
    - Once chilled, churn the custard base in an ice cream maker according to the manufacturer's instructions until it reaches a soft-serve consistency.
9. **Freeze:**
    - Transfer the churned Butter Tart Ice Cream to an airtight container, smoothing the top. Cover and freeze for at least 4 hours or until firm before serving.
10. **Serve:**
    - Scoop the Butter Tart Ice Cream into bowls or cones and enjoy the rich, caramelized flavors of butter tarts in every creamy bite!

This recipe captures the essence of butter tarts in a delightful frozen dessert, perfect for enjoying as a nostalgic treat or introducing the classic Canadian flavors to new audiences. Adjust the sweetness and nuttiness according to your taste preferences for a truly satisfying Butter Tart Ice Cream experience.

Timbit Ice Cream (inspired by Tim Hortons' Timbits)

Ingredients:

- 1 cup heavy cream
- 1 cup whole milk
- 1/2 cup granulated sugar
- 4 large egg yolks
- 1 teaspoon vanilla extract
- 1 cup chopped Timbits (assorted flavors)
- 1/4 cup chocolate glaze or fudge sauce (optional, for extra sweetness)

Instructions:

1. **Prepare the Custard Base:**
   - In a medium saucepan, heat the heavy cream, whole milk, and granulated sugar over medium heat, stirring occasionally, until the mixture begins to steam. Do not let it boil.
2. **Whisk Egg Yolks:**
   - In a separate bowl, whisk the egg yolks until smooth. Gradually pour about half of the hot cream mixture into the egg yolks, whisking constantly to temper the eggs.
3. **Combine and Cook:**
   - Pour the tempered egg mixture back into the saucepan with the remaining cream mixture. Cook over medium heat, stirring constantly with a wooden spoon or spatula, until the mixture thickens and coats the back of the spoon (about 170°F on an instant-read thermometer).
4. **Add Vanilla and Timbits:**
   - Remove from heat and stir in the vanilla extract. Let the mixture cool to room temperature.
   - Once cooled, stir in the chopped Timbits until evenly distributed. If desired, swirl in chocolate glaze or fudge sauce for extra sweetness and flavor.
5. **Chill the Mixture:**
   - Cover the mixture and refrigerate for at least 4 hours or until completely chilled.
6. **Churn the Ice Cream:**
   - Once chilled, churn the custard base in an ice cream maker according to the manufacturer's instructions until it reaches a soft-serve consistency.
7. **Freeze:**

- Transfer the churned Timbit Ice Cream to an airtight container, smoothing the top. Cover and freeze for at least 4 hours or until firm before serving.
8. **Serve:**
    - Scoop the Timbit Ice Cream into bowls or cones and enjoy the nostalgic flavors of Timbits in every creamy bite!

This recipe captures the essence of Timbits in a delightful frozen treat, perfect for enjoying the flavors of Canada's favorite donut holes in a new and refreshing way. Adjust the mix-ins and sweetness according to your preference for a personalized Timbit Ice Cream experience.

Maple Bacon Ice Cream

Ingredients:

- 1 cup heavy cream
- 1 cup whole milk
- 1/2 cup pure maple syrup
- 1/2 cup granulated sugar
- 4 large egg yolks
- 1 teaspoon vanilla extract
- 1/2 cup cooked bacon, chopped into small pieces
- Maple syrup for drizzling (optional)

Instructions:

1. **Prepare the Custard Base:**
    - In a medium saucepan, heat the heavy cream, whole milk, maple syrup, and granulated sugar over medium heat, stirring occasionally, until the mixture begins to steam. Do not let it boil.
2. **Whisk Egg Yolks:**
    - In a separate bowl, whisk the egg yolks until smooth. Gradually pour about half of the hot cream mixture into the egg yolks, whisking constantly to temper the eggs.
3. **Combine and Cook:**
    - Pour the tempered egg mixture back into the saucepan with the remaining cream mixture. Cook over medium heat, stirring constantly with a wooden spoon or spatula, until the mixture thickens and coats the back of the spoon (about 170°F on an instant-read thermometer).
4. **Add Vanilla and Bacon:**
    - Remove from heat and stir in the vanilla extract. Let the mixture cool to room temperature.
    - Once cooled, stir in the chopped cooked bacon until evenly distributed.
5. **Chill the Mixture:**
    - Cover the mixture and refrigerate for at least 4 hours or until completely chilled.
6. **Churn the Ice Cream:**
    - Once chilled, churn the custard base in an ice cream maker according to the manufacturer's instructions until it reaches a soft-serve consistency.
7. **Freeze:**

- Transfer the churned Maple Bacon Ice Cream to an airtight container, smoothing the top. Drizzle with additional maple syrup if desired for extra flavor.
8. **Final Freeze:**
    - Cover and freeze for at least 4 hours or until firm before serving.
9. **Serve:**
    - Scoop the Maple Bacon Ice Cream into bowls or cones and enjoy the unique blend of sweet maple syrup with salty, crispy bacon pieces!

This recipe offers a delightful twist on traditional ice cream flavors by combining the richness of maple syrup with the savory crunch of bacon, creating a decadent and satisfying dessert experience. Adjust the sweetness and bacon amount according to your taste preferences for a perfect balance of flavors.

Smoked Salmon Ice Cream

Ingredients:

- 1 cup heavy cream
- 1 cup whole milk
- 1/2 cup smoked salmon, finely chopped
- 4 large egg yolks
- 1/2 cup granulated sugar
- 1 teaspoon lemon zest
- 1 tablespoon lemon juice
- 1/4 teaspoon black pepper
- Pinch of salt
- Fresh dill, chopped (for garnish)

Instructions:

1. **Prepare the Smoked Salmon:**
   - Finely chop the smoked salmon and set it aside.
2. **Prepare the Custard Base:**
   - In a medium saucepan, heat the heavy cream, whole milk, and granulated sugar over medium heat, stirring occasionally, until the mixture begins to steam. Do not let it boil.
3. **Whisk Egg Yolks:**
   - In a separate bowl, whisk the egg yolks until smooth. Gradually pour about half of the hot cream mixture into the egg yolks, whisking constantly to temper the eggs.
4. **Combine and Cook:**
   - Pour the tempered egg mixture back into the saucepan with the remaining cream mixture. Cook over medium heat, stirring constantly with a wooden spoon or spatula, until the mixture thickens and coats the back of the spoon (about 170°F on an instant-read thermometer).
5. **Add Lemon Zest, Lemon Juice, Black Pepper, and Salt:**
   - Remove from heat and stir in the lemon zest, lemon juice, black pepper, and a pinch of salt. Mix until well combined.
6. **Cool the Mixture:**
   - Stir in the chopped smoked salmon. Let the mixture cool to room temperature.
7. **Chill the Mixture:**

- Cover the mixture and refrigerate for at least 4 hours or until completely chilled.
8. **Churn the Ice Cream:**
     - Once chilled, churn the custard base in an ice cream maker according to the manufacturer's instructions until it reaches a soft-serve consistency.
9. **Freeze:**
     - Transfer the churned Smoked Salmon Ice Cream to an airtight container, smoothing the top. Cover and freeze for at least 4 hours or until firm before serving.
10. **Serve:**
     - Scoop the Smoked Salmon Ice Cream into bowls or cones. Garnish with fresh chopped dill before serving for an added touch of freshness.

This recipe offers a unique and savory twist on ice cream, perfect for those who enjoy adventurous flavors. The combination of creamy texture with smoky salmon and a hint of citrus makes for a sophisticated and unexpected dessert experience. Adjust the seasoning and lemon to taste for a personalized flavor profile.

Nanaimo Bar Ice Cream

Ingredients:

For the Custard Base:

- 1 cup heavy cream
- 1 cup whole milk
- 1/2 cup granulated sugar
- 4 large egg yolks
- 1 teaspoon vanilla extract

For the Nanaimo Bar Mix-ins:

- 1/2 cup chocolate crumbs (graham cracker crumbs mixed with cocoa powder)
- 1/2 cup shredded coconut
- 1/2 cup chopped walnuts or pecans
- 1/4 cup chocolate chips or chunks

For the Chocolate Ganache Swirl:

- 1/2 cup dark chocolate chips
- 1/4 cup heavy cream

Instructions:

1. **Prepare the Custard Base:**
   - In a medium saucepan, heat the heavy cream, whole milk, and granulated sugar over medium heat, stirring occasionally, until the mixture begins to steam. Do not let it boil.
2. **Whisk Egg Yolks:**
   - In a separate bowl, whisk the egg yolks until smooth. Gradually pour about half of the hot cream mixture into the egg yolks, whisking constantly to temper the eggs.
3. **Combine and Cook:**
   - Pour the tempered egg mixture back into the saucepan with the remaining cream mixture. Cook over medium heat, stirring constantly with a wooden spoon or spatula, until the mixture thickens and coats the back of the spoon (about 170°F on an instant-read thermometer).
4. **Add Vanilla Extract:**

- Remove from heat and stir in the vanilla extract. Let the mixture cool to room temperature.
5. **Prepare the Nanaimo Bar Mix-ins:**
    - In a bowl, combine the chocolate crumbs, shredded coconut, chopped nuts, and chocolate chips.
6. **Prepare the Chocolate Ganache Swirl:**
    - In a microwave-safe bowl or small saucepan, heat the dark chocolate chips and heavy cream until melted and smooth. Stir until well combined.
7. **Assemble the Ice Cream:**
    - Once the custard base has cooled, fold in the Nanaimo Bar mix-ins until evenly distributed.
    - Drizzle the chocolate ganache over the ice cream mixture and gently swirl it with a spoon or spatula to create a marbled effect.
8. **Chill the Mixture:**
    - Cover the ice cream mixture and refrigerate for at least 4 hours or until completely chilled.
9. **Churn the Ice Cream:**
    - Once chilled, churn the custard base in an ice cream maker according to the manufacturer's instructions until it reaches a soft-serve consistency.
10. **Freeze:**
    - Transfer the churned Nanaimo Bar Ice Cream to an airtight container, smoothing the top. Cover and freeze for at least 4 hours or until firm before serving.
11. **Serve:**
    - Scoop the Nanaimo Bar Ice Cream into bowls or cones and enjoy the layers of chocolate, coconut, and nuts reminiscent of the classic Nanaimo Bar!

This recipe captures the flavors and textures of Nanaimo Bar in a frozen dessert, offering a delightful twist on a Canadian favorite. Adjust the mix-ins and chocolate ganache swirl according to your preference for a personalized Nanaimo Bar Ice Cream experience.

Moose Tracks Ice Cream

Ingredients:

- 1 cup heavy cream
- 1 cup whole milk
- 1/2 cup granulated sugar
- 4 large egg yolks
- 1 teaspoon vanilla extract
- 1/2 cup fudge sauce or chocolate syrup
- 1/2 cup mini peanut butter cups, chopped into small pieces

Instructions:

1. **Prepare the Custard Base:**
   - In a medium saucepan, heat the heavy cream, whole milk, and granulated sugar over medium heat, stirring occasionally, until the mixture begins to steam. Do not let it boil.
2. **Whisk Egg Yolks:**
   - In a separate bowl, whisk the egg yolks until smooth. Gradually pour about half of the hot cream mixture into the egg yolks, whisking constantly to temper the eggs.
3. **Combine and Cook:**
   - Pour the tempered egg mixture back into the saucepan with the remaining cream mixture. Cook over medium heat, stirring constantly with a wooden spoon or spatula, until the mixture thickens and coats the back of the spoon (about 170°F on an instant-read thermometer).
4. **Add Vanilla Extract:**
   - Remove from heat and stir in the vanilla extract. Let the mixture cool to room temperature.
5. **Chill the Mixture:**
   - Cover the mixture and refrigerate for at least 4 hours or until completely chilled.
6. **Churn the Ice Cream:**
   - Once chilled, churn the custard base in an ice cream maker according to the manufacturer's instructions until it reaches a soft-serve consistency.
7. **Add Fudge Sauce and Peanut Butter Cups:**
   - During the last minute of churning, add the fudge sauce or chocolate syrup and chopped mini peanut butter cups to the ice cream. Let them mix evenly.

8. **Freeze:**
    - Transfer the churned Moose Tracks Ice Cream to an airtight container, smoothing the top. Cover and freeze for at least 4 hours or until firm before serving.
9. **Serve:**
    - Scoop the Moose Tracks Ice Cream into bowls or cones and enjoy the creamy vanilla base with swirls of fudge and delightful bites of mini peanut butter cups!

This homemade Moose Tracks Ice Cream recipe captures the essence of the classic store-bought favorite, allowing you to customize the amount of fudge sauce and peanut butter cups to your liking. It's a delicious treat perfect for any ice cream lover.

Saskatoon Berry Pie Ice Cream

Ingredients:

- 1 cup heavy cream
- 1 cup whole milk
- 1/2 cup granulated sugar
- 4 large egg yolks
- 1 teaspoon vanilla extract
- 1 cup Saskatoon berries, fresh or frozen
- 1/4 cup brown sugar
- 1 tablespoon lemon juice
- 1/2 cup graham cracker crumbs

Instructions:

1. **Prepare the Saskatoon Berry Mixture:**
   - In a small saucepan, combine Saskatoon berries, brown sugar, and lemon juice. Cook over medium heat, stirring occasionally, until the berries break down and release their juices, about 8-10 minutes. Remove from heat and let cool.
2. **Prepare the Custard Base:**
   - In a medium saucepan, heat the heavy cream, whole milk, and granulated sugar over medium heat, stirring occasionally, until the mixture begins to steam. Do not let it boil.
3. **Whisk Egg Yolks:**
   - In a separate bowl, whisk the egg yolks until smooth. Gradually pour about half of the hot cream mixture into the egg yolks, whisking constantly to temper the eggs.
4. **Combine and Cook:**
   - Pour the tempered egg mixture back into the saucepan with the remaining cream mixture. Cook over medium heat, stirring constantly with a wooden spoon or spatula, until the mixture thickens and coats the back of the spoon (about 170°F on an instant-read thermometer).
5. **Add Vanilla Extract:**
   - Remove from heat and stir in the vanilla extract. Let the mixture cool to room temperature.
6. **Combine the Custard and Saskatoon Berry Mixture:**
   - Stir the cooled Saskatoon berry mixture and graham cracker crumbs into the custard base until evenly distributed.

7. **Chill the Mixture:**
   - Cover the mixture and refrigerate for at least 4 hours or until completely chilled.
8. **Churn the Ice Cream:**
   - Once chilled, churn the custard base in an ice cream maker according to the manufacturer's instructions until it reaches a soft-serve consistency.
9. **Freeze:**
   - Transfer the churned Saskatoon Berry Pie Ice Cream to an airtight container, smoothing the top. Cover and freeze for at least 4 hours or until firm before serving.
10. **Serve:**
    - Scoop the Saskatoon Berry Pie Ice Cream into bowls or cones and enjoy the delicious blend of creamy vanilla with sweet Saskatoon berries and graham cracker crumbs!

This recipe captures the essence of Saskatoon Berry Pie in a refreshing ice cream form, perfect for summer or any time you crave a taste of this Canadian favorite. Adjust the sweetness and texture according to your preference for a perfect Saskatoon Berry Pie Ice Cream experience.

Blueberry Pancake Ice Cream

Ingredients:

- 1 cup heavy cream
- 1 cup whole milk
- 1/2 cup granulated sugar
- 4 large egg yolks
- 1 teaspoon vanilla extract
- 1 cup fresh or frozen blueberries
- 1/4 cup maple syrup
- 1 cup pancake pieces (recipe below)

For the Pancake Pieces:

- 1 cup all-purpose flour
- 1 tablespoon granulated sugar
- 2 teaspoons baking powder
- 1/4 teaspoon salt
- 1 large egg
- 1 cup milk
- 2 tablespoons unsalted butter, melted
- 1 teaspoon vanilla extract

Instructions:

1. **Prepare the Pancake Pieces:**
    - In a large bowl, whisk together the flour, sugar, baking powder, and salt.
    - In another bowl, whisk the egg, milk, melted butter, and vanilla extract until well combined.
    - Pour the wet ingredients into the dry ingredients and stir until just combined. Do not overmix; the batter should be slightly lumpy.
    - Heat a non-stick skillet or griddle over medium heat and lightly grease with butter or cooking spray.
    - Pour about 1/4 cup of batter onto the skillet for each pancake. Cook until bubbles form on the surface of the pancake and the edges look set, about 2-3 minutes. Flip and cook for another 1-2 minutes until golden brown.
    - Transfer the cooked pancakes to a cutting board and let cool. Cut the pancakes into small pieces.
2. **Prepare the Blueberry Sauce:**

- In a small saucepan, combine the blueberries and maple syrup. Cook over medium heat, stirring occasionally, until the blueberries burst and release their juices, about 5-7 minutes. Remove from heat and let cool.

3. **Prepare the Custard Base:**
   - In a medium saucepan, heat the heavy cream, whole milk, and granulated sugar over medium heat, stirring occasionally, until the mixture begins to steam. Do not let it boil.
4. **Whisk Egg Yolks:**
   - In a separate bowl, whisk the egg yolks until smooth. Gradually pour about half of the hot cream mixture into the egg yolks, whisking constantly to temper the eggs.
5. **Combine and Cook:**
   - Pour the tempered egg mixture back into the saucepan with the remaining cream mixture. Cook over medium heat, stirring constantly with a wooden spoon or spatula, until the mixture thickens and coats the back of the spoon (about 170°F on an instant-read thermometer).
6. **Add Vanilla Extract and Assemble:**
   - Remove from heat and stir in the vanilla extract. Let the mixture cool to room temperature.
   - Once cooled, stir in the blueberry sauce, pancake pieces, and any remaining maple syrup until evenly distributed.
7. **Chill the Mixture:**
   - Cover the mixture and refrigerate for at least 4 hours or until completely chilled.
8. **Churn the Ice Cream:**
   - Once chilled, churn the custard base in an ice cream maker according to the manufacturer's instructions until it reaches a soft-serve consistency.
9. **Freeze:**
   - Transfer the churned Blueberry Pancake Ice Cream to an airtight container, smoothing the top. Cover and freeze for at least 4 hours or until firm before serving.
10. **Serve:**
    - Scoop the Blueberry Pancake Ice Cream into bowls or cones and enjoy the delicious blend of creamy vanilla with bursts of sweet blueberries and pancake pieces!

This recipe captures the flavors of a comforting breakfast in a refreshing ice cream form, perfect for summer mornings or as a special dessert treat. Adjust the sweetness and pancake pieces according to your preference for a delightful Blueberry Pancake Ice Cream experience.

Blueberry Pancake Ice Cream

Ingredients:

- 1 cup heavy cream
- 1 cup whole milk
- 1/2 cup granulated sugar
- 4 large egg yolks
- 1 teaspoon vanilla extract
- 1 cup fresh or frozen blueberries
- 1/4 cup maple syrup
- 1 cup pancake pieces (recipe below)

For the Pancake Pieces:

- 1 cup all-purpose flour
- 1 tablespoon granulated sugar
- 2 teaspoons baking powder
- 1/4 teaspoon salt
- 1 large egg
- 1 cup milk
- 2 tablespoons unsalted butter, melted
- 1 teaspoon vanilla extract

Instructions:

1. **Prepare the Pancake Pieces:**
    - In a large bowl, whisk together the flour, sugar, baking powder, and salt.
    - In another bowl, whisk the egg, milk, melted butter, and vanilla extract until well combined.
    - Pour the wet ingredients into the dry ingredients and stir until just combined. Do not overmix; the batter should be slightly lumpy.
    - Heat a non-stick skillet or griddle over medium heat and lightly grease with butter or cooking spray.
    - Pour about 1/4 cup of batter onto the skillet for each pancake. Cook until bubbles form on the surface of the pancake and the edges look set, about 2-3 minutes. Flip and cook for another 1-2 minutes until golden brown.
    - Transfer the cooked pancakes to a cutting board and let cool. Cut the pancakes into small pieces.
2. **Prepare the Blueberry Sauce:**

- In a small saucepan, combine the blueberries and maple syrup. Cook over medium heat, stirring occasionally, until the blueberries burst and release their juices, about 5-7 minutes. Remove from heat and let cool.

3. **Prepare the Custard Base:**
   - In a medium saucepan, heat the heavy cream, whole milk, and granulated sugar over medium heat, stirring occasionally, until the mixture begins to steam. Do not let it boil.

4. **Whisk Egg Yolks:**
   - In a separate bowl, whisk the egg yolks until smooth. Gradually pour about half of the hot cream mixture into the egg yolks, whisking constantly to temper the eggs.

5. **Combine and Cook:**
   - Pour the tempered egg mixture back into the saucepan with the remaining cream mixture. Cook over medium heat, stirring constantly with a wooden spoon or spatula, until the mixture thickens and coats the back of the spoon (about 170°F on an instant-read thermometer).

6. **Add Vanilla Extract and Assemble:**
   - Remove from heat and stir in the vanilla extract. Let the mixture cool to room temperature.
   - Once cooled, stir in the blueberry sauce, pancake pieces, and any remaining maple syrup until evenly distributed.

7. **Chill the Mixture:**
   - Cover the mixture and refrigerate for at least 4 hours or until completely chilled.

8. **Churn the Ice Cream:**
   - Once chilled, churn the custard base in an ice cream maker according to the manufacturer's instructions until it reaches a soft-serve consistency.

9. **Freeze:**
   - Transfer the churned Blueberry Pancake Ice Cream to an airtight container, smoothing the top. Cover and freeze for at least 4 hours or until firm before serving.

10. **Serve:**
    - Scoop the Blueberry Pancake Ice Cream into bowls or cones and enjoy the delicious blend of creamy vanilla with bursts of sweet blueberries and pancake pieces!

This recipe captures the flavors of a comforting breakfast in a refreshing ice cream form, perfect for summer mornings or as a special dessert treat. Adjust the sweetness and pancake pieces according to your preference for a delightful Blueberry Pancake Ice Cream experience.

Beavertail Pastry Ice Cream

Ingredients:

- 1 cup heavy cream
- 1 cup whole milk
- 1/2 cup granulated sugar
- 4 large egg yolks
- 1 teaspoon vanilla extract
- 1/4 teaspoon ground cinnamon
- 1/2 cup Beavertail pastry pieces (recipe below)

For the Beavertail Pastry Pieces:

- 1 sheet store-bought puff pastry, thawed
- 1/4 cup unsalted butter, melted
- 1/4 cup granulated sugar
- 1 teaspoon ground cinnamon

Instructions:

1. **Prepare the Beavertail Pastry Pieces:**
   - Preheat your oven to 400°F (200°C) and line a baking sheet with parchment paper.
   - Roll out the thawed puff pastry on a lightly floured surface into a rectangle about 1/4-inch thick.
   - Brush the melted butter evenly over the surface of the puff pastry.
   - In a small bowl, mix together the granulated sugar and ground cinnamon. Sprinkle this mixture evenly over the buttered puff pastry.
   - Fold the puff pastry in half lengthwise and press lightly to seal. Cut the pastry into strips about 1 inch wide.
   - Twist each strip gently and place them on the prepared baking sheet.
   - Bake in the preheated oven for 12-15 minutes, or until golden brown and puffed. Remove from oven and let cool completely. Once cooled, break or chop into small pieces.
2. **Prepare the Custard Base:**
   - In a medium saucepan, heat the heavy cream, whole milk, and granulated sugar over medium heat, stirring occasionally, until the mixture begins to steam. Do not let it boil.
3. **Whisk Egg Yolks:**

- In a separate bowl, whisk the egg yolks until smooth. Gradually pour about half of the hot cream mixture into the egg yolks, whisking constantly to temper the eggs.

4. **Combine and Cook:**
    - Pour the tempered egg mixture back into the saucepan with the remaining cream mixture. Cook over medium heat, stirring constantly with a wooden spoon or spatula, until the mixture thickens and coats the back of the spoon (about 170°F on an instant-read thermometer).

5. **Add Vanilla Extract and Cinnamon:**
    - Remove from heat and stir in the vanilla extract and ground cinnamon. Let the mixture cool to room temperature.

6. **Assemble the Ice Cream:**
    - Once cooled, stir in the Beavertail pastry pieces until evenly distributed.

7. **Chill the Mixture:**
    - Cover the mixture and refrigerate for at least 4 hours or until completely chilled.

8. **Churn the Ice Cream:**
    - Once chilled, churn the custard base in an ice cream maker according to the manufacturer's instructions until it reaches a soft-serve consistency.

9. **Freeze:**
    - Transfer the churned Beavertail Pastry Ice Cream to an airtight container, smoothing the top. Cover and freeze for at least 4 hours or until firm before serving.

10. **Serve:**
    - Scoop the Beavertail Pastry Ice Cream into bowls or cones and enjoy the delicious blend of cinnamon-sugar pastry goodness in every creamy bite!

This recipe captures the essence of Beavertail pastries in a delightful frozen dessert, perfect for enjoying the flavors of Canada's favorite treat in a new and refreshing way. Adjust the cinnamon-sugar ratio and pastry pieces according to your taste preferences for a truly satisfying Beavertail Pastry Ice Cream experience.

Poutine Ice Cream

Ingredients:

- 1 cup heavy cream
- 1 cup whole milk
- 1/2 cup granulated sugar
- 4 large egg yolks
- 1 teaspoon vanilla extract
- 1/2 cup cheese curds, chopped into small pieces
- 1/2 cup French fries, chopped into small pieces
- 1/4 cup gravy sauce (recipe below)

For the Gravy Sauce:

- 2 tablespoons unsalted butter
- 2 tablespoons all-purpose flour
- 1 cup beef or chicken broth
- Salt and pepper to taste

Instructions:

1. **Prepare the Gravy Sauce:**
   - In a small saucepan, melt the butter over medium heat. Add the flour and cook, stirring constantly, for about 1 minute to make a roux.
   - Gradually whisk in the broth, stirring constantly to avoid lumps. Bring to a boil, then reduce the heat and simmer until the gravy thickens, about 5-7 minutes.
   - Season with salt and pepper to taste. Remove from heat and let cool completely.
2. **Prepare the Custard Base:**
   - In a medium saucepan, heat the heavy cream, whole milk, and granulated sugar over medium heat, stirring occasionally, until the mixture begins to steam. Do not let it boil.
3. **Whisk Egg Yolks:**
   - In a separate bowl, whisk the egg yolks until smooth. Gradually pour about half of the hot cream mixture into the egg yolks, whisking constantly to temper the eggs.
4. **Combine and Cook:**

- Pour the tempered egg mixture back into the saucepan with the remaining cream mixture. Cook over medium heat, stirring constantly with a wooden spoon or spatula, until the mixture thickens and coats the back of the spoon (about 170°F on an instant-read thermometer).

5. **Add Vanilla Extract and Assemble:**
    - Remove from heat and stir in the vanilla extract. Let the mixture cool to room temperature.
    - Once cooled, stir in the cheese curds and French fries pieces until evenly distributed.
    - Swirl in the cooled gravy sauce to taste, creating a marbled effect.

6. **Chill the Mixture:**
    - Cover the mixture and refrigerate for at least 4 hours or until completely chilled.

7. **Churn the Ice Cream:**
    - Once chilled, churn the custard base in an ice cream maker according to the manufacturer's instructions until it reaches a soft-serve consistency.

8. **Freeze:**
    - Transfer the churned Poutine Ice Cream to an airtight container, smoothing the top. Cover and freeze for at least 4 hours or until firm before serving.

9. **Serve:**
    - Scoop the Poutine Ice Cream into bowls or cones and enjoy the playful blend of savory cheese curds, crispy French fries, and gravy in a creamy dessert form!

This recipe offers a whimsical take on a beloved Canadian dish, perfect for those who enjoy creative culinary experiments. Adjust the amount of cheese curds, French fries, and gravy sauce according to your taste preferences for a unique and memorable Poutine Ice Cream experience.

Butter Tart Ice Cream

Ingredients:

- 1 cup heavy cream
- 1 cup whole milk
- 1/2 cup granulated sugar
- 4 large egg yolks
- 1 teaspoon vanilla extract
- 1/2 cup butter tart filling (recipe below)
- 1/2 cup pecans, toasted and chopped

For the Butter Tart Filling:

- 1/2 cup packed brown sugar
- 1/4 cup unsalted butter, melted
- 1/4 cup corn syrup
- 1 large egg
- 1 teaspoon vanilla extract
- Pinch of salt

Instructions:

1. **Prepare the Butter Tart Filling:**
   - In a bowl, whisk together brown sugar, melted butter, corn syrup, egg, vanilla extract, and a pinch of salt until well combined.
2. **Cook the Filling:**
   - Transfer the mixture to a small saucepan. Cook over medium heat, stirring constantly, until it thickens slightly (about 5-7 minutes). Remove from heat and let cool completely.
3. **Prepare the Custard Base:**
   - In a medium saucepan, heat the heavy cream, whole milk, and granulated sugar over medium heat, stirring occasionally, until the mixture begins to steam. Do not let it boil.
4. **Whisk Egg Yolks:**
   - In a separate bowl, whisk the egg yolks until smooth. Gradually pour about half of the hot cream mixture into the egg yolks, whisking constantly to temper the eggs.
5. **Combine and Cook:**

- Pour the tempered egg mixture back into the saucepan with the remaining cream mixture. Cook over medium heat, stirring constantly with a wooden spoon or spatula, until the mixture thickens and coats the back of the spoon (about 170°F on an instant-read thermometer).
6. **Add Vanilla Extract and Butter Tart Filling:**
    - Remove from heat and stir in the vanilla extract. Let the mixture cool to room temperature.
    - Once cooled, stir in the prepared butter tart filling and chopped pecans until evenly distributed.
7. **Chill the Mixture:**
    - Cover the mixture and refrigerate for at least 4 hours or until completely chilled.
8. **Churn the Ice Cream:**
    - Once chilled, churn the custard base in an ice cream maker according to the manufacturer's instructions until it reaches a soft-serve consistency.
9. **Freeze:**
    - Transfer the churned Butter Tart Ice Cream to an airtight container, smoothing the top. Cover and freeze for at least 4 hours or until firm before serving.
10. **Serve:**
    - Scoop the Butter Tart Ice Cream into bowls or cones and enjoy the rich, caramelized flavors of butter tart and crunchy pecans in every creamy bite!

This recipe captures the essence of traditional butter tarts in a delightful frozen dessert, perfect for enjoying the flavors of Canada's beloved pastry in a new and refreshing way. Adjust the sweetness and pecan ratio according to your taste preferences for a truly satisfying Butter Tart Ice Cream experience.

Coffee Crisp Ice Cream

Ingredients:

- 1 cup heavy cream
- 1 cup whole milk
- 1/2 cup granulated sugar
- 4 large egg yolks
- 1 teaspoon vanilla extract
- 1/4 cup instant coffee granules
- 1 cup chocolate-covered wafer bars (like Coffee Crisp), chopped into small pieces

Instructions:

1. **Prepare the Custard Base:**
    - In a medium saucepan, heat the heavy cream, whole milk, instant coffee granules, and granulated sugar over medium heat, stirring occasionally, until the mixture begins to steam. Do not let it boil.
2. **Whisk Egg Yolks:**
    - In a separate bowl, whisk the egg yolks until smooth. Gradually pour about half of the hot cream mixture into the egg yolks, whisking constantly to temper the eggs.
3. **Combine and Cook:**
    - Pour the tempered egg mixture back into the saucepan with the remaining cream mixture. Cook over medium heat, stirring constantly with a wooden spoon or spatula, until the mixture thickens and coats the back of the spoon (about 170°F on an instant-read thermometer).
4. **Add Vanilla Extract:**
    - Remove from heat and stir in the vanilla extract. Let the mixture cool to room temperature.
5. **Chill the Mixture:**
    - Cover the mixture and refrigerate for at least 4 hours or until completely chilled.
6. **Churn the Ice Cream:**
    - Once chilled, churn the custard base in an ice cream maker according to the manufacturer's instructions until it reaches a soft-serve consistency.
7. **Add Coffee Crisp Pieces:**
    - During the last minute of churning, add the chopped Coffee Crisp pieces to the ice cream. Let them mix evenly.

8. **Freeze:**
    - Transfer the churned Coffee Crisp Ice Cream to an airtight container, smoothing the top. Cover and freeze for at least 4 hours or until firm before serving.
9. **Serve:**
    - Scoop the Coffee Crisp Ice Cream into bowls or cones and enjoy the delightful blend of coffee-flavored ice cream with crunchy chocolate-covered wafer pieces!

This recipe captures the essence of Coffee Crisp bars in a refreshing ice cream form, perfect for coffee and chocolate lovers alike. Adjust the amount of instant coffee and Coffee Crisp pieces according to your taste preferences for a perfect Coffee Crisp Ice Cream experience.

Tiger Tail Ice Cream

Ingredients:

- 1 cup heavy cream
- 1 cup whole milk
- 1/2 cup granulated sugar
- 4 large egg yolks
- 1 teaspoon vanilla extract
- Zest of 1 orange
- 1/4 cup orange juice
- 1 tablespoon orange liqueur (optional)
- 1/2 teaspoon anise extract or 1 tablespoon black licorice syrup
- Orange food coloring (optional)
- 1/2 cup black licorice candy, chopped into small pieces

Instructions:

1. **Prepare the Custard Base:**
   - In a medium saucepan, heat the heavy cream, whole milk, orange zest, and granulated sugar over medium heat, stirring occasionally, until the mixture begins to steam. Do not let it boil.
2. **Whisk Egg Yolks:**
   - In a separate bowl, whisk the egg yolks until smooth. Gradually pour about half of the hot cream mixture into the egg yolks, whisking constantly to temper the eggs.
3. **Combine and Cook:**
   - Pour the tempered egg mixture back into the saucepan with the remaining cream mixture. Cook over medium heat, stirring constantly with a wooden spoon or spatula, until the mixture thickens and coats the back of the spoon (about 170°F on an instant-read thermometer).
4. **Add Flavorings:**
   - Remove from heat and stir in the vanilla extract, orange juice, orange liqueur (if using), and anise extract or black licorice syrup. Add orange food coloring if desired to achieve a vibrant orange color.
5. **Chill the Mixture:**
   - Cover the mixture and refrigerate for at least 4 hours or until completely chilled.
6. **Churn the Ice Cream:**

- Once chilled, churn the custard base in an ice cream maker according to the manufacturer's instructions until it reaches a soft-serve consistency.
7. **Add Licorice Pieces:**
   - During the last minute of churning, add the chopped black licorice candy to the ice cream. Let them mix evenly.
8. **Freeze:**
   - Transfer the churned Tiger Tail Ice Cream to an airtight container, smoothing the top. Cover and freeze for at least 4 hours or until firm before serving.
9. **Serve:**
   - Scoop the Tiger Tail Ice Cream into bowls or cones and enjoy the unique combination of orange and licorice flavors in a creamy frozen dessert!

This recipe captures the distinctive taste of Tiger Tail Ice Cream, a favorite in Canada. Adjust the intensity of orange and licorice flavors according to your preference for a delightful homemade treat reminiscent of this classic Canadian flavor.

Nanaimo Bar Ice Cream

Ingredients:

- 1 cup heavy cream
- 1 cup whole milk
- 1/2 cup granulated sugar
- 4 large egg yolks
- 1 teaspoon vanilla extract
- 1/2 cup chocolate ganache or fudge sauce (recipe below)
- 1/2 cup shredded coconut, toasted
- 1/2 cup chopped walnuts, toasted
- 1/2 cup graham cracker crumbs

For the Chocolate Ganache or Fudge Sauce:

- 1/2 cup heavy cream
- 1 cup semi-sweet chocolate chips
- 2 tablespoons unsalted butter

Instructions:

1. **Prepare the Chocolate Ganache or Fudge Sauce:**
    - In a small saucepan, heat the heavy cream over medium heat until it just begins to simmer.
    - Remove from heat and add the chocolate chips and butter. Let sit for 1-2 minutes, then stir until smooth and glossy. Set aside to cool.
2. **Prepare the Custard Base:**
    - In a medium saucepan, heat the heavy cream, whole milk, and granulated sugar over medium heat, stirring occasionally, until the mixture begins to steam. Do not let it boil.
3. **Whisk Egg Yolks:**
    - In a separate bowl, whisk the egg yolks until smooth. Gradually pour about half of the hot cream mixture into the egg yolks, whisking constantly to temper the eggs.
4. **Combine and Cook:**
    - Pour the tempered egg mixture back into the saucepan with the remaining cream mixture. Cook over medium heat, stirring constantly with a wooden spoon or spatula, until the mixture thickens and coats the back of the spoon (about 170°F on an instant-read thermometer).

5. **Add Vanilla Extract and Assemble:**
    - Remove from heat and stir in the vanilla extract. Let the mixture cool to room temperature.
    - Once cooled, stir in the chocolate ganache or fudge sauce, toasted shredded coconut, chopped walnuts, and graham cracker crumbs until evenly distributed.
6. **Chill the Mixture:**
    - Cover the mixture and refrigerate for at least 4 hours or until completely chilled.
7. **Churn the Ice Cream:**
    - Once chilled, churn the custard base in an ice cream maker according to the manufacturer's instructions until it reaches a soft-serve consistency.
8. **Freeze:**
    - Transfer the churned Nanaimo Bar Ice Cream to an airtight container, smoothing the top. Cover and freeze for at least 4 hours or until firm before serving.
9. **Serve:**
    - Scoop the Nanaimo Bar Ice Cream into bowls or cones and enjoy the delightful combination of chocolate, coconut, and nuts in every creamy bite!

This recipe captures the flavors and textures of Nanaimo Bars in a delicious frozen dessert, perfect for celebrating Canadian culinary heritage. Adjust the amount of chocolate ganache, coconut, walnuts, and graham cracker crumbs according to your taste preferences for a satisfying Nanaimo Bar Ice Cream experience.

Maple Walnut Ice Cream

Ingredients:

- 1 cup heavy cream
- 1 cup whole milk
- 1/2 cup pure maple syrup
- 1/2 cup chopped toasted walnuts
- 4 large egg yolks
- 1 teaspoon vanilla extract
- Pinch of salt

Instructions:

1. **Prepare the Custard Base:**
   - In a medium saucepan, combine the heavy cream, whole milk, and maple syrup. Heat over medium heat, stirring occasionally, until the mixture begins to steam. Do not let it boil.
2. **Whisk Egg Yolks:**
   - In a separate bowl, whisk the egg yolks until smooth.
3. **Temper the Eggs:**
   - Gradually pour about half of the hot cream mixture into the egg yolks, whisking constantly to temper the eggs.
4. **Combine and Cook:**
   - Pour the tempered egg mixture back into the saucepan with the remaining cream mixture. Cook over medium heat, stirring constantly with a wooden spoon or spatula, until the mixture thickens and coats the back of the spoon (about 170°F on an instant-read thermometer).
5. **Add Vanilla and Salt:**
   - Remove from heat and stir in the vanilla extract and a pinch of salt. Let the mixture cool to room temperature.
6. **Chill the Mixture:**
   - Cover the mixture and refrigerate for at least 4 hours or until completely chilled.
7. **Toast Walnuts:**
   - While the ice cream base is chilling, toast the chopped walnuts in a dry skillet over medium heat for 5-7 minutes, stirring frequently, until fragrant and lightly browned. Let them cool completely.
8. **Churn the Ice Cream:**

- Once chilled, churn the custard base in an ice cream maker according to the manufacturer's instructions until it reaches a soft-serve consistency.

9. **Add Walnuts:**
    - During the last minute of churning, add the toasted chopped walnuts to the ice cream. Let them mix evenly.
10. **Freeze:**
    - Transfer the churned Maple Walnut Ice Cream to an airtight container, smoothing the top. Cover and freeze for at least 4 hours or until firm before serving.
11. **Serve:**
    - Scoop the Maple Walnut Ice Cream into bowls or cones and enjoy the delightful blend of creamy maple sweetness and crunchy toasted walnuts!

This recipe captures the essence of Canadian maple syrup and walnuts in a delicious frozen dessert, perfect for enjoying the flavors of Canada in a refreshing and creamy form. Adjust the sweetness and nuttiness according to your taste preferences for a perfect Maple Walnut Ice Cream experience.

Cherry Blossom Ice Cream

Ingredients:

- 1 cup heavy cream
- 1 cup whole milk
- 1/2 cup granulated sugar
- 4 large egg yolks
- 1 teaspoon vanilla extract
- 1/2 cup cherry preserves or cherry jam
- 1/2 cup chopped maraschino cherries
- 1/4 cup chopped dark chocolate or chocolate chips

Instructions:

1. **Prepare the Custard Base:**
    - In a medium saucepan, heat the heavy cream, whole milk, and granulated sugar over medium heat, stirring occasionally, until the mixture begins to steam. Do not let it boil.
2. **Whisk Egg Yolks:**
    - In a separate bowl, whisk the egg yolks until smooth.
3. **Temper the Eggs:**
    - Gradually pour about half of the hot cream mixture into the egg yolks, whisking constantly to temper the eggs.
4. **Combine and Cook:**
    - Pour the tempered egg mixture back into the saucepan with the remaining cream mixture. Cook over medium heat, stirring constantly with a wooden spoon or spatula, until the mixture thickens and coats the back of the spoon (about 170°F on an instant-read thermometer).
5. **Add Vanilla Extract:**
    - Remove from heat and stir in the vanilla extract. Let the mixture cool to room temperature.
6. **Chill the Mixture:**
    - Cover the mixture and refrigerate for at least 4 hours or until completely chilled.
7. **Prepare Cherry Swirl:**
    - In a small bowl, mix together the cherry preserves or cherry jam with the chopped maraschino cherries.
8. **Churn the Ice Cream:**

- Once chilled, churn the custard base in an ice cream maker according to the manufacturer's instructions until it reaches a soft-serve consistency.

9. **Add Cherry Swirl and Chocolate:**
   - During the last minute of churning, add the cherry mixture and chopped dark chocolate or chocolate chips to the ice cream. Let them mix evenly.
10. **Freeze:**
    - Transfer the churned Cherry Blossom Ice Cream to an airtight container, smoothing the top. Cover and freeze for at least 4 hours or until firm before serving.
11. **Serve:**
    - Scoop the Cherry Blossom Ice Cream into bowls or cones and enjoy the delightful blend of cherry flavors and chocolate in every creamy bite!

This recipe captures the essence of cherry blossom season with a creamy twist, perfect for enjoying the floral and fruity flavors in a refreshing ice cream. Adjust the sweetness and amount of cherries according to your taste preferences for a perfect Cherry Blossom Ice Cream experience.

Nanaimo Bar Ice Cream

Ingredients:

- 1 cup heavy cream
- 1 cup whole milk
- 1/2 cup granulated sugar
- 4 large egg yolks
- 1 teaspoon vanilla extract
- 1/2 cup chocolate ganache or fudge sauce (recipe below)
- 1/2 cup shredded coconut, toasted
- 1/2 cup chopped walnuts, toasted
- 1/2 cup graham cracker crumbs

For the Chocolate Ganache or Fudge Sauce:

- 1/2 cup heavy cream
- 1 cup semi-sweet chocolate chips
- 2 tablespoons unsalted butter

Instructions:

1. **Prepare the Chocolate Ganache or Fudge Sauce:**
   - In a small saucepan, heat the heavy cream over medium heat until it just begins to simmer.
   - Remove from heat and add the chocolate chips and butter. Let sit for 1-2 minutes, then stir until smooth and glossy. Set aside to cool.
2. **Prepare the Custard Base:**
   - In a medium saucepan, heat the heavy cream, whole milk, and granulated sugar over medium heat, stirring occasionally, until the mixture begins to steam. Do not let it boil.
3. **Whisk Egg Yolks:**
   - In a separate bowl, whisk the egg yolks until smooth. Gradually pour about half of the hot cream mixture into the egg yolks, whisking constantly to temper the eggs.
4. **Combine and Cook:**
   - Pour the tempered egg mixture back into the saucepan with the remaining cream mixture. Cook over medium heat, stirring constantly with a wooden spoon or spatula, until the mixture thickens and coats the back of the spoon (about 170°F on an instant-read thermometer).

5. **Add Vanilla Extract and Assemble:**
    - Remove from heat and stir in the vanilla extract. Let the mixture cool to room temperature.
    - Once cooled, stir in the chocolate ganache or fudge sauce, toasted shredded coconut, chopped walnuts, and graham cracker crumbs until evenly distributed.
6. **Chill the Mixture:**
    - Cover the mixture and refrigerate for at least 4 hours or until completely chilled.
7. **Churn the Ice Cream:**
    - Once chilled, churn the custard base in an ice cream maker according to the manufacturer's instructions until it reaches a soft-serve consistency.
8. **Freeze:**
    - Transfer the churned Nanaimo Bar Ice Cream to an airtight container, smoothing the top. Cover and freeze for at least 4 hours or until firm before serving.
9. **Serve:**
    - Scoop the Nanaimo Bar Ice Cream into bowls or cones and enjoy the delightful combination of chocolate, coconut, and nuts in every creamy bite!

This recipe captures the flavors and textures of Nanaimo Bars in a delicious frozen dessert, perfect for celebrating Canadian culinary heritage. Adjust the amount of chocolate ganache, coconut, walnuts, and graham cracker crumbs according to your taste preferences for a satisfying Nanaimo Bar Ice Cream experience.

Saskatoon Berry Ice Cream

Ingredients:

- 1 cup heavy cream
- 1 cup whole milk
- 1/2 cup granulated sugar
- 4 large egg yolks
- 1 teaspoon vanilla extract
- 1 cup Saskatoon berries, fresh or frozen
- 1/4 cup Saskatoon berry jam or preserves

Instructions:

1. **Prepare the Saskatoon Berry Puree:**
   - In a blender or food processor, puree the Saskatoon berries until smooth. If using fresh berries, you may need to strain the puree to remove seeds.
2. **Prepare the Custard Base:**
   - In a medium saucepan, combine the heavy cream, whole milk, and granulated sugar. Heat over medium heat, stirring occasionally, until the mixture begins to steam. Do not let it boil.
3. **Whisk Egg Yolks:**
   - In a separate bowl, whisk the egg yolks until smooth.
4. **Temper the Eggs:**
   - Gradually pour about half of the hot cream mixture into the egg yolks, whisking constantly to temper the eggs.
5. **Combine and Cook:**
   - Pour the tempered egg mixture back into the saucepan with the remaining cream mixture. Cook over medium heat, stirring constantly with a wooden spoon or spatula, until the mixture thickens and coats the back of the spoon (about 170°F on an instant-read thermometer).
6. **Add Vanilla Extract and Saskatoon Berry Puree:**
   - Remove from heat and stir in the vanilla extract. Let the mixture cool to room temperature.
   - Once cooled, stir in the Saskatoon berry puree and Saskatoon berry jam or preserves until evenly distributed.
7. **Chill the Mixture:**
   - Cover the mixture and refrigerate for at least 4 hours or until completely chilled.
8. **Churn the Ice Cream:**

- Once chilled, churn the custard base in an ice cream maker according to the manufacturer's instructions until it reaches a soft-serve consistency.
9. **Freeze:**
   - Transfer the churned Saskatoon Berry Ice Cream to an airtight container, smoothing the top. Cover and freeze for at least 4 hours or until firm before serving.
10. **Serve:**
    - Scoop the Saskatoon Berry Ice Cream into bowls or cones and enjoy the unique and delightful flavor of Canadian Saskatoon berries in a creamy frozen dessert!

This recipe captures the essence of Saskatoon berries in a refreshing ice cream, perfect for enjoying the flavors of Canadian cuisine. Adjust the sweetness and intensity of the berry flavor according to your taste preferences for a perfect Saskatoon Berry Ice Cream experience.

Maple Butter Tart Ice Cream

Ingredients:

- 1 cup heavy cream
- 1 cup whole milk
- 1/2 cup pure maple syrup
- 1/2 cup chopped pecans, toasted
- 4 large egg yolks
- 1 teaspoon vanilla extract
- 1/4 cup butter, melted
- 1/2 cup packed brown sugar
- Pinch of salt

Instructions:

1. **Prepare the Custard Base:**
   - In a medium saucepan, combine the heavy cream, whole milk, and pure maple syrup. Heat over medium heat, stirring occasionally, until the mixture begins to steam. Do not let it boil.
2. **Toast Pecans:**
   - While the cream mixture is heating, toast the chopped pecans in a dry skillet over medium heat for 5-7 minutes, stirring frequently, until fragrant and lightly browned. Set aside to cool.
3. **Prepare the Butter Tart Filling:**
   - In a separate saucepan, melt the butter over medium heat. Stir in the brown sugar and a pinch of salt. Cook, stirring constantly, until the mixture starts to bubble and thicken slightly (about 2-3 minutes). Remove from heat and let cool slightly.
4. **Whisk Egg Yolks:**
   - In a separate bowl, whisk the egg yolks until smooth.
5. **Combine and Cook:**
   - Gradually pour about half of the hot cream mixture into the egg yolks, whisking constantly to temper the eggs.
   - Pour the tempered egg mixture back into the saucepan with the remaining cream mixture. Cook over medium heat, stirring constantly with a wooden spoon or spatula, until the mixture thickens and coats the back of the spoon (about 170°F on an instant-read thermometer).
6. **Add Vanilla Extract and Butter Tart Filling:**

- Remove from heat and stir in the vanilla extract. Let the mixture cool to room temperature.
- Once cooled, stir in the melted butter and brown sugar mixture (butter tart filling) until well combined.

7. **Chill the Mixture:**
   - Cover the mixture and refrigerate for at least 4 hours or until completely chilled.
8. **Churn the Ice Cream:**
   - Once chilled, churn the custard base in an ice cream maker according to the manufacturer's instructions until it reaches a soft-serve consistency.
9. **Add Toasted Pecans:**
   - During the last minute of churning, add the toasted chopped pecans to the ice cream. Let them mix evenly.
10. **Freeze:**
    - Transfer the churned Maple Butter Tart Ice Cream to an airtight container, smoothing the top. Cover and freeze for at least 4 hours or until firm before serving.
11. **Serve:**
    - Scoop the Maple Butter Tart Ice Cream into bowls or cones and enjoy the delightful blend of maple syrup, buttery caramel, and toasted pecans in every creamy bite!

This recipe captures the essence of Maple Butter Tarts in a delicious frozen dessert, perfect for celebrating Canadian flavors in a unique and satisfying way. Adjust the sweetness and nuttiness according to your taste preferences for a perfect Maple Butter Tart Ice Cream experience.

Butter Tart Ice Cream

Ingredients:

- 1 cup heavy cream
- 1 cup whole milk
- 1/2 cup packed brown sugar
- 4 large egg yolks
- 1 teaspoon vanilla extract
- 1/2 cup chopped pecans, toasted
- 1/4 cup butter, melted
- 1/4 cup maple syrup (optional, for added flavor)
- Pinch of salt

Instructions:

1. **Prepare the Custard Base:**
   - In a medium saucepan, combine the heavy cream, whole milk, and packed brown sugar. Heat over medium heat, stirring occasionally, until the mixture begins to steam. Do not let it boil.
2. **Toast Pecans:**
   - While the cream mixture is heating, toast the chopped pecans in a dry skillet over medium heat for 5-7 minutes, stirring frequently, until fragrant and lightly browned. Set aside to cool.
3. **Prepare the Butter Tart Filling:**
   - In a separate saucepan, melt the butter over medium heat. Stir in the maple syrup (if using) and a pinch of salt. Cook, stirring constantly, until the mixture starts to bubble and thicken slightly (about 2-3 minutes). Remove from heat and let cool slightly.
4. **Whisk Egg Yolks:**
   - In a separate bowl, whisk the egg yolks until smooth.
5. **Combine and Cook:**
   - Gradually pour about half of the hot cream mixture into the egg yolks, whisking constantly to temper the eggs.
   - Pour the tempered egg mixture back into the saucepan with the remaining cream mixture. Cook over medium heat, stirring constantly with a wooden spoon or spatula, until the mixture thickens and coats the back of the spoon (about 170°F on an instant-read thermometer).
6. **Add Vanilla Extract and Butter Tart Filling:**

- Remove from heat and stir in the vanilla extract. Let the mixture cool to room temperature.
- Once cooled, stir in the melted butter and brown sugar mixture (butter tart filling) until well combined.

7. **Chill the Mixture:**
   - Cover the mixture and refrigerate for at least 4 hours or until completely chilled.
8. **Churn the Ice Cream:**
   - Once chilled, churn the custard base in an ice cream maker according to the manufacturer's instructions until it reaches a soft-serve consistency.
9. **Add Toasted Pecans:**
   - During the last minute of churning, add the toasted chopped pecans to the ice cream. Let them mix evenly.
10. **Freeze:**
    - Transfer the churned Butter Tart Ice Cream to an airtight container, smoothing the top. Cover and freeze for at least 4 hours or until firm before serving.
11. **Serve:**
    - Scoop the Butter Tart Ice Cream into bowls or cones and enjoy the rich caramel and buttery flavors with the crunch of toasted pecans in every creamy bite!

This recipe brings the beloved Butter Tart flavors into a delightful frozen dessert, perfect for enjoying the iconic Canadian treat in a new and refreshing way. Adjust the sweetness and nuttiness according to your taste preferences for a perfect Butter Tart Ice Cream experience.

Blueberry Grunt Ice Cream

Ingredients:

- 1 cup heavy cream
- 1 cup whole milk
- 1/2 cup granulated sugar
- 4 large egg yolks
- 1 teaspoon vanilla extract
- 1 cup fresh or frozen blueberries
- 1/4 cup maple syrup (optional, for added flavor)
- 1 tablespoon lemon juice
- Pinch of salt

Instructions:

1. **Prepare the Blueberry Compote:**
   - In a saucepan, combine the blueberries, maple syrup (if using), lemon juice, and a pinch of salt. Cook over medium heat, stirring occasionally, until the blueberries release their juices and soften (about 5-7 minutes). Mash some of the berries with a fork or potato masher to thicken the compote. Remove from heat and let cool.
2. **Prepare the Custard Base:**
   - In a medium saucepan, combine the heavy cream, whole milk, and granulated sugar. Heat over medium heat, stirring occasionally, until the mixture begins to steam. Do not let it boil.
3. **Whisk Egg Yolks:**
   - In a separate bowl, whisk the egg yolks until smooth.
4. **Temper the Eggs:**
   - Gradually pour about half of the hot cream mixture into the egg yolks, whisking constantly to temper the eggs.
5. **Combine and Cook:**
   - Pour the tempered egg mixture back into the saucepan with the remaining cream mixture. Cook over medium heat, stirring constantly with a wooden spoon or spatula, until the mixture thickens and coats the back of the spoon (about 170°F on an instant-read thermometer).
6. **Add Vanilla Extract and Blueberry Compote:**
   - Remove from heat and stir in the vanilla extract. Let the mixture cool to room temperature.

- Once cooled, gently fold in the cooled blueberry compote until it swirls through the ice cream base.
7. **Chill the Mixture:**
   - Cover the mixture and refrigerate for at least 4 hours or until completely chilled.
8. **Churn the Ice Cream:**
   - Once chilled, churn the custard base in an ice cream maker according to the manufacturer's instructions until it reaches a soft-serve consistency.
9. **Freeze:**
   - Transfer the churned Blueberry Grunt Ice Cream to an airtight container, smoothing the top. Cover and freeze for at least 4 hours or until firm before serving.
10. **Serve:**
    - Scoop the Blueberry Grunt Ice Cream into bowls or cones and enjoy the delightful blend of creamy ice cream with swirls of blueberry compote!

This recipe captures the comforting flavors of blueberry grunt in a cool and refreshing dessert. Adjust the sweetness and tartness of the compote according to your taste preferences for a perfect Blueberry Grunt Ice Cream experience.

Nova Scotia Blueberry Ice Cream

Ingredients:

- 1 cup heavy cream
- 1 cup whole milk
- 1/2 cup granulated sugar
- 4 large egg yolks
- 1 teaspoon vanilla extract
- 1 cup fresh Nova Scotia blueberries
- 1/4 cup maple syrup (optional, for added flavor)
- 1 tablespoon lemon juice
- Pinch of salt

Instructions:

1. **Prepare the Blueberry Compote:**
   - In a saucepan, combine the Nova Scotia blueberries, maple syrup (if using), lemon juice, and a pinch of salt. Cook over medium heat, stirring occasionally, until the blueberries release their juices and soften (about 5-7 minutes). Mash some of the berries with a fork or potato masher to thicken the compote. Remove from heat and let cool.
2. **Prepare the Custard Base:**
   - In a medium saucepan, combine the heavy cream, whole milk, and granulated sugar. Heat over medium heat, stirring occasionally, until the mixture begins to steam. Do not let it boil.
3. **Whisk Egg Yolks:**
   - In a separate bowl, whisk the egg yolks until smooth.
4. **Temper the Eggs:**
   - Gradually pour about half of the hot cream mixture into the egg yolks, whisking constantly to temper the eggs.
5. **Combine and Cook:**
   - Pour the tempered egg mixture back into the saucepan with the remaining cream mixture. Cook over medium heat, stirring constantly with a wooden spoon or spatula, until the mixture thickens and coats the back of the spoon (about 170°F on an instant-read thermometer).
6. **Add Vanilla Extract and Blueberry Compote:**
   - Remove from heat and stir in the vanilla extract. Let the mixture cool to room temperature.

- Once cooled, gently fold in the cooled Nova Scotia blueberry compote until it swirls through the ice cream base.
7. **Chill the Mixture:**
    - Cover the mixture and refrigerate for at least 4 hours or until completely chilled.
8. **Churn the Ice Cream:**
    - Once chilled, churn the custard base in an ice cream maker according to the manufacturer's instructions until it reaches a soft-serve consistency.
9. **Freeze:**
    - Transfer the churned Nova Scotia Blueberry Ice Cream to an airtight container, smoothing the top. Cover and freeze for at least 4 hours or until firm before serving.
10. **Serve:**
    - Scoop the Nova Scotia Blueberry Ice Cream into bowls or cones and enjoy the delightful flavor of fresh blueberries from Nova Scotia in every creamy bite!

This recipe highlights the natural sweetness and tartness of Nova Scotia blueberries in a refreshing frozen dessert. Adjust the sweetness and tartness of the compote according to your taste preferences for a perfect Nova Scotia Blueberry Ice Cream experience.

Atlantic Lobster Ice Cream (a novelty flavor)

Ingredients:

- 1 cup heavy cream
- 1 cup whole milk
- 1/2 cup granulated sugar
- 4 large egg yolks
- 1 teaspoon vanilla extract
- 1 cup cooked Atlantic lobster meat, chopped finely
- 1/4 cup lobster broth or seafood stock
- 1/4 teaspoon salt
- 1/8 teaspoon ground black pepper
- Optional: 1 tablespoon brandy or cognac (for a touch of richness)

Instructions:

1. **Prepare the Lobster Mixture:**
   - In a small saucepan, heat the lobster broth or seafood stock over medium heat until simmering. Add the finely chopped lobster meat and cook for 2-3 minutes until heated through. Remove from heat and let cool.
2. **Prepare the Custard Base:**
   - In a medium saucepan, combine the heavy cream, whole milk, and granulated sugar. Heat over medium heat, stirring occasionally, until the mixture begins to steam. Do not let it boil.
3. **Whisk Egg Yolks:**
   - In a separate bowl, whisk the egg yolks until smooth.
4. **Temper the Eggs:**
   - Gradually pour about half of the hot cream mixture into the egg yolks, whisking constantly to temper the eggs.
5. **Combine and Cook:**
   - Pour the tempered egg mixture back into the saucepan with the remaining cream mixture. Cook over medium heat, stirring constantly with a wooden spoon or spatula, until the mixture thickens and coats the back of the spoon (about 170°F on an instant-read thermometer).
6. **Add Vanilla Extract and Lobster Mixture:**
   - Remove from heat and stir in the vanilla extract, salt, and black pepper. Let the mixture cool to room temperature.

- Once cooled, gently fold in the cooled lobster mixture until evenly distributed throughout the ice cream base. Optionally, add brandy or cognac for additional flavor.

7. **Chill the Mixture:**
   - Cover the mixture and refrigerate for at least 4 hours or until completely chilled.
8. **Churn the Ice Cream:**
   - Once chilled, churn the custard base in an ice cream maker according to the manufacturer's instructions until it reaches a soft-serve consistency.
9. **Freeze:**
   - Transfer the churned Atlantic Lobster Ice Cream to an airtight container, smoothing the top. Cover and freeze for at least 4 hours or until firm before serving.
10. **Serve:**
    - Scoop the Atlantic Lobster Ice Cream into bowls or cones and enjoy the unique and savory flavor of lobster in a creamy frozen dessert!

This recipe offers a novel twist on ice cream flavors, incorporating the savory notes of Atlantic lobster for those looking to explore adventurous culinary experiences. Adjust seasoning and optional ingredients according to your taste preferences for a perfect Atlantic Lobster Ice Cream experience.

Maritime Donair Ice Cream

Ingredients:

- 1 cup heavy cream
- 1 cup whole milk
- 1/2 cup granulated sugar
- 4 large egg yolks
- 1 teaspoon vanilla extract
- 1/2 cup sweetened condensed milk
- 1/2 cup donair meat, finely chopped or shredded
- 2 tablespoons donair sauce (recipe below)
- Pinch of salt

For the Donair Sauce:

- 1/2 cup sweetened condensed milk
- 1/4 cup white vinegar
- 1/2 teaspoon garlic powder
- 1/4 teaspoon onion powder
- Pinch of salt

Instructions:

1. **Prepare the Donair Sauce:**
   - In a bowl, whisk together the sweetened condensed milk, white vinegar, garlic powder, onion powder, and a pinch of salt until smooth. Adjust vinegar to taste for desired tanginess. Set aside.
2. **Prepare the Custard Base:**
   - In a medium saucepan, combine the heavy cream, whole milk, and granulated sugar. Heat over medium heat, stirring occasionally, until the mixture begins to steam. Do not let it boil.
3. **Whisk Egg Yolks:**
   - In a separate bowl, whisk the egg yolks until smooth.
4. **Temper the Eggs:**
   - Gradually pour about half of the hot cream mixture into the egg yolks, whisking constantly to temper the eggs.
5. **Combine and Cook:**
   - Pour the tempered egg mixture back into the saucepan with the remaining cream mixture. Cook over medium heat, stirring constantly with a wooden

spoon or spatula, until the mixture thickens and coats the back of the spoon (about 170°F on an instant-read thermometer).
6. **Add Vanilla Extract, Sweetened Condensed Milk, and Donair Sauce:**
    - Remove from heat and stir in the vanilla extract and sweetened condensed milk until well combined.
    - Once cooled slightly, fold in the chopped or shredded donair meat and donair sauce until evenly distributed throughout the ice cream base.
7. **Chill the Mixture:**
    - Cover the mixture and refrigerate for at least 4 hours or until completely chilled.
8. **Churn the Ice Cream:**
    - Once chilled, churn the custard base in an ice cream maker according to the manufacturer's instructions until it reaches a soft-serve consistency.
9. **Freeze:**
    - Transfer the churned Maritime Donair Ice Cream to an airtight container, smoothing the top. Cover and freeze for at least 4 hours or until firm before serving.
10. **Serve:**
    - Scoop the Maritime Donair Ice Cream into bowls or cones and enjoy the unique and savory flavors of a Maritime donair in a creamy frozen dessert!

This recipe captures the essence of Maritime donair, blending savory meat and tangy sauce into a refreshing ice cream. Adjust the sweetness and seasoning according to your taste preferences for a perfect Maritime Donair Ice Cream experience.

Nova Scotia Apple Crisp Ice Cream

Ingredients:

- 1 cup heavy cream
- 1 cup whole milk
- 1/2 cup granulated sugar
- 4 large egg yolks
- 1 teaspoon vanilla extract
- 1 cup Nova Scotia apples, peeled, cored, and diced
- 2 tablespoons unsalted butter
- 1/4 cup brown sugar
- 1/2 teaspoon ground cinnamon
- Pinch of salt
- 1/2 cup crisp oatmeal topping (optional, for garnish)

Instructions:

1. **Prepare the Apple Mixture:**
   - In a skillet, melt the unsalted butter over medium heat. Add the diced Nova Scotia apples, brown sugar, ground cinnamon, and a pinch of salt. Cook, stirring occasionally, until the apples are tender and caramelized (about 8-10 minutes). Remove from heat and let cool.
2. **Prepare the Custard Base:**
   - In a medium saucepan, combine the heavy cream, whole milk, and granulated sugar. Heat over medium heat, stirring occasionally, until the mixture begins to steam. Do not let it boil.
3. **Whisk Egg Yolks:**
   - In a separate bowl, whisk the egg yolks until smooth.
4. **Temper the Eggs:**
   - Gradually pour about half of the hot cream mixture into the egg yolks, whisking constantly to temper the eggs.
5. **Combine and Cook:**
   - Pour the tempered egg mixture back into the saucepan with the remaining cream mixture. Cook over medium heat, stirring constantly with a wooden spoon or spatula, until the mixture thickens and coats the back of the spoon (about 170°F on an instant-read thermometer).
6. **Add Vanilla Extract and Apple Mixture:**
   - Remove from heat and stir in the vanilla extract. Let the mixture cool to room temperature.

- Once cooled, gently fold in the cooled apple mixture until it swirls through the ice cream base.
7. **Chill the Mixture:**
    - Cover the mixture and refrigerate for at least 4 hours or until completely chilled.
8. **Churn the Ice Cream:**
    - Once chilled, churn the custard base in an ice cream maker according to the manufacturer's instructions until it reaches a soft-serve consistency.
9. **Freeze:**
    - Transfer the churned Nova Scotia Apple Crisp Ice Cream to an airtight container, smoothing the top. Sprinkle the crisp oatmeal topping over the top if desired. Cover and freeze for at least 4 hours or until firm before serving.
10. **Serve:**
    - Scoop the Nova Scotia Apple Crisp Ice Cream into bowls or cones and enjoy the comforting flavors of apple crisp in a creamy frozen dessert!

This recipe captures the essence of Nova Scotia's apple crisp in a delightful frozen treat, perfect for enjoying the flavors of fall year-round. Adjust the sweetness and cinnamon spice according to your taste preferences for a perfect Nova Scotia Apple Crisp Ice Cream experience.

Quebec Maple Pudding Ice Cream

Ingredients:

- 1 cup heavy cream
- 1 cup whole milk
- 1/2 cup granulated sugar
- 4 large egg yolks
- 1 teaspoon vanilla extract
- 1/2 cup pure Quebec maple syrup
- 1/4 teaspoon salt
- Maple candies or maple sugar (optional, for garnish)

Instructions:

1. **Prepare the Custard Base:**
    - In a medium saucepan, combine the heavy cream, whole milk, and granulated sugar. Heat over medium heat, stirring occasionally, until the mixture begins to steam. Do not let it boil.
2. **Whisk Egg Yolks:**
    - In a separate bowl, whisk the egg yolks until smooth.
3. **Temper the Eggs:**
    - Gradually pour about half of the hot cream mixture into the egg yolks, whisking constantly to temper the eggs.
4. **Combine and Cook:**
    - Pour the tempered egg mixture back into the saucepan with the remaining cream mixture. Cook over medium heat, stirring constantly with a wooden spoon or spatula, until the mixture thickens and coats the back of the spoon (about 170°F on an instant-read thermometer).
5. **Add Vanilla Extract and Maple Syrup:**
    - Remove from heat and stir in the vanilla extract, Quebec maple syrup, and salt. Let the mixture cool to room temperature.
6. **Chill the Mixture:**
    - Cover the mixture and refrigerate for at least 4 hours or until completely chilled.
7. **Churn the Ice Cream:**
    - Once chilled, churn the custard base in an ice cream maker according to the manufacturer's instructions until it reaches a soft-serve consistency.
8. **Freeze:**

- Transfer the churned Quebec Maple Pudding Ice Cream to an airtight container. Cover and freeze for at least 4 hours or until firm before serving.
9. **Serve:**
    - Scoop the Quebec Maple Pudding Ice Cream into bowls or cones. Optionally, garnish with maple candies or maple sugar for added sweetness and texture.

Enjoy the creamy, maple-infused goodness of Quebec Maple Pudding Ice Cream, capturing the essence of Canadian maple syrup in every spoonful! Adjust the sweetness of the maple syrup according to your taste preferences for a perfect dessert.

PEI Potato Ice Cream

Ingredients:

- 1 cup heavy cream
- 1 cup whole milk
- 1/2 cup granulated sugar
- 4 large egg yolks
- 1 teaspoon vanilla extract
- 1 cup mashed PEI potatoes, cooled
- 1/4 teaspoon salt
- Optional: 1/4 cup maple syrup or honey (for added sweetness)

Instructions:

1. **Prepare the Mashed PEI Potatoes:**
   - Peel, chop, and boil PEI potatoes until tender. Drain well and mash until smooth. Let cool completely.
2. **Prepare the Custard Base:**
   - In a medium saucepan, combine the heavy cream, whole milk, and granulated sugar. Heat over medium heat, stirring occasionally, until the mixture begins to steam. Do not let it boil.
3. **Whisk Egg Yolks:**
   - In a separate bowl, whisk the egg yolks until smooth.
4. **Temper the Eggs:**
   - Gradually pour about half of the hot cream mixture into the egg yolks, whisking constantly to temper the eggs.
5. **Combine and Cook:**
   - Pour the tempered egg mixture back into the saucepan with the remaining cream mixture. Cook over medium heat, stirring constantly with a wooden spoon or spatula, until the mixture thickens and coats the back of the spoon (about 170°F on an instant-read thermometer).
6. **Add Vanilla Extract and Mashed PEI Potatoes:**
   - Remove from heat and stir in the vanilla extract, mashed PEI potatoes, and salt. If using, add maple syrup or honey for added sweetness. Mix until well combined.
7. **Chill the Mixture:**
   - Cover the mixture and refrigerate for at least 4 hours or until completely chilled.
8. **Churn the Ice Cream:**

- Once chilled, churn the custard base in an ice cream maker according to the manufacturer's instructions until it reaches a soft-serve consistency.

9. **Freeze:**
    - Transfer the churned PEI Potato Ice Cream to an airtight container. Cover and freeze for at least 4 hours or until firm before serving.
10. **Serve:**
    - Scoop the PEI Potato Ice Cream into bowls or cones and enjoy the unique creamy texture and subtle potato flavor from Prince Edward Island!

This recipe highlights the natural sweetness and creamy texture of PEI potatoes in a delightful frozen dessert. Adjust the sweetness and seasoning according to your taste preferences for a perfect PEI Potato Ice Cream experience.

Butter Tart Ice Cream

Ingredients:

- 1 cup heavy cream
- 1 cup whole milk
- 1/2 cup packed brown sugar
- 4 large egg yolks
- 1 teaspoon vanilla extract
- 1/4 cup butter, melted
- 1/2 cup chopped pecans (optional, for added texture)
- 1/2 cup raisins (optional, for added flavor)
- Pinch of salt

Instructions:

1. **Prepare the Custard Base:**
    - In a medium saucepan, combine the heavy cream, whole milk, and brown sugar. Heat over medium heat, stirring occasionally, until the mixture begins to steam. Do not let it boil.
2. **Whisk Egg Yolks:**
    - In a separate bowl, whisk the egg yolks until smooth.
3. **Temper the Eggs:**
    - Gradually pour about half of the hot cream mixture into the egg yolks, whisking constantly to temper the eggs.
4. **Combine and Cook:**
    - Pour the tempered egg mixture back into the saucepan with the remaining cream mixture. Cook over medium heat, stirring constantly with a wooden spoon or spatula, until the mixture thickens and coats the back of the spoon (about 170°F on an instant-read thermometer).
5. **Add Vanilla Extract, Butter, Pecans, and Raisins:**
    - Remove from heat and stir in the vanilla extract, melted butter, chopped pecans (if using), raisins (if using), and a pinch of salt. Mix until well combined.
6. **Chill the Mixture:**
    - Cover the mixture and refrigerate for at least 4 hours or until completely chilled.
7. **Churn the Ice Cream:**
    - Once chilled, churn the custard base in an ice cream maker according to the manufacturer's instructions until it reaches a soft-serve consistency.

8. **Freeze:**
    - Transfer the churned Butter Tart Ice Cream to an airtight container. Cover and freeze for at least 4 hours or until firm before serving.
9. **Serve:**
    - Scoop the Butter Tart Ice Cream into bowls or cones and enjoy the delicious caramel flavors and buttery goodness reminiscent of traditional butter tarts!

This recipe captures the essence of butter tarts in a cool and creamy dessert. Adjust the amount of pecans and raisins according to your preference for texture and flavor. Enjoy this Canadian-inspired treat any time of the year!

Saskatoon Berry Ice Cream

Ingredients:

- 1 cup heavy cream
- 1 cup whole milk
- 1/2 cup granulated sugar
- 4 large egg yolks
- 1 teaspoon vanilla extract
- 1 cup fresh or frozen Saskatoon berries
- 1/4 cup Saskatoon berry jam or preserves
- Pinch of salt

Instructions:

1. **Prepare the Saskatoon Berry Mixture:**
    - In a saucepan, combine the Saskatoon berries and Saskatoon berry jam (or preserves) over medium heat. Cook, stirring occasionally, until the berries soften and release their juices (about 5-7 minutes). Remove from heat and let cool slightly.
2. **Prepare the Custard Base:**
    - In a medium saucepan, combine the heavy cream, whole milk, and granulated sugar. Heat over medium heat, stirring occasionally, until the mixture begins to steam. Do not let it boil.
3. **Whisk Egg Yolks:**
    - In a separate bowl, whisk the egg yolks until smooth.
4. **Temper the Eggs:**
    - Gradually pour about half of the hot cream mixture into the egg yolks, whisking constantly to temper the eggs.
5. **Combine and Cook:**
    - Pour the tempered egg mixture back into the saucepan with the remaining cream mixture. Cook over medium heat, stirring constantly with a wooden spoon or spatula, until the mixture thickens and coats the back of the spoon (about 170°F on an instant-read thermometer).
6. **Add Vanilla Extract and Saskatoon Berry Mixture:**
    - Remove from heat and stir in the vanilla extract. Let the mixture cool slightly.
    - Once cooled slightly, gently fold in the cooled Saskatoon berry mixture until it swirls through the ice cream base.
7. **Chill the Mixture:**

- Cover the mixture and refrigerate for at least 4 hours or until completely chilled.
8. **Churn the Ice Cream:**
    - Once chilled, churn the custard base in an ice cream maker according to the manufacturer's instructions until it reaches a soft-serve consistency.
9. **Freeze:**
    - Transfer the churned Saskatoon Berry Ice Cream to an airtight container, smoothing the top. Cover and freeze for at least 4 hours or until firm before serving.
10. **Serve:**
    - Scoop the Saskatoon Berry Ice Cream into bowls or cones and enjoy the deliciously unique flavor of Saskatoon berries in a creamy frozen dessert!

This recipe captures the natural sweetness and distinctive flavor of Saskatoon berries, perfect for enjoying the flavors of the Canadian prairies in a refreshing ice cream. Adjust the sweetness of the Saskatoon berry mixture according to your taste preferences for a perfect Saskatoon Berry Ice Cream experience.

Canadian Bacon Ice Cream

Ingredients:

- 1 cup heavy cream
- 1 cup whole milk
- 1/2 cup granulated sugar
- 4 large egg yolks
- 1 teaspoon vanilla extract
- 1/2 cup Canadian bacon, finely chopped
- Maple syrup or maple extract (optional, for added flavor)
- Pinch of salt

Instructions:

1. **Prepare the Canadian Bacon:**
     - In a skillet over medium heat, cook the finely chopped Canadian bacon until crispy. Remove from heat and let cool on paper towels to absorb excess grease. Once cooled, chop into smaller pieces.
2. **Prepare the Custard Base:**
     - In a medium saucepan, combine the heavy cream, whole milk, and granulated sugar. Heat over medium heat, stirring occasionally, until the mixture begins to steam. Do not let it boil.
3. **Whisk Egg Yolks:**
     - In a separate bowl, whisk the egg yolks until smooth.
4. **Temper the Eggs:**
     - Gradually pour about half of the hot cream mixture into the egg yolks, whisking constantly to temper the eggs.
5. **Combine and Cook:**
     - Pour the tempered egg mixture back into the saucepan with the remaining cream mixture. Cook over medium heat, stirring constantly with a wooden spoon or spatula, until the mixture thickens and coats the back of the spoon (about 170°F on an instant-read thermometer).
6. **Add Vanilla Extract, Canadian Bacon, and Maple Syrup/Extract:**
     - Remove from heat and stir in the vanilla extract. Let the mixture cool slightly.
     - Once cooled slightly, gently fold in the cooled Canadian bacon pieces. Optionally, add a splash of maple syrup or a few drops of maple extract for added flavor.
7. **Chill the Mixture:**

- Cover the mixture and refrigerate for at least 4 hours or until completely chilled.
8. **Churn the Ice Cream:**
    - Once chilled, churn the custard base in an ice cream maker according to the manufacturer's instructions until it reaches a soft-serve consistency.
9. **Freeze:**
    - Transfer the churned Canadian Bacon Ice Cream to an airtight container, smoothing the top. Cover and freeze for at least 4 hours or until firm before serving.
10. **Serve:**
    - Scoop the Canadian Bacon Ice Cream into bowls or cones and enjoy the savory and creamy flavors of Canadian bacon in a unique frozen dessert!

This recipe offers a savory twist on traditional sweet ice cream, perfect for those who enjoy experimenting with unexpected flavor combinations. Adjust the sweetness and maple flavor according to your taste preferences for a perfect Canadian Bacon Ice Cream experience.

Butter Tart Ice Cream

Ingredients:

- 1 cup heavy cream
- 1 cup whole milk
- 1/2 cup packed brown sugar
- 4 large egg yolks
- 1 teaspoon vanilla extract
- 1/4 cup butter, melted
- 1/2 cup chopped pecans
- 1/2 cup raisins
- Pinch of salt

Instructions:

1. **Prepare the Custard Base:**
    - In a medium saucepan, combine the heavy cream, whole milk, and brown sugar. Heat over medium heat, stirring occasionally, until the mixture begins to steam. Do not let it boil.
2. **Whisk Egg Yolks:**
    - In a separate bowl, whisk the egg yolks until smooth.
3. **Temper the Eggs:**
    - Gradually pour about half of the hot cream mixture into the egg yolks, whisking constantly to temper the eggs.
4. **Combine and Cook:**
    - Pour the tempered egg mixture back into the saucepan with the remaining cream mixture. Cook over medium heat, stirring constantly with a wooden spoon or spatula, until the mixture thickens and coats the back of the spoon (about 170°F on an instant-read thermometer).
5. **Add Vanilla Extract, Butter, Pecans, Raisins, and Salt:**
    - Remove from heat and stir in the vanilla extract, melted butter, chopped pecans, raisins, and a pinch of salt. Mix until well combined.
6. **Chill the Mixture:**
    - Cover the mixture and refrigerate for at least 4 hours or until completely chilled.
7. **Churn the Ice Cream:**
    - Once chilled, churn the custard base in an ice cream maker according to the manufacturer's instructions until it reaches a soft-serve consistency.
8. **Freeze:**

- Transfer the churned Butter Tart Ice Cream to an airtight container, smoothing the top. Cover and freeze for at least 4 hours or until firm before serving.
9. **Serve:**
    - Scoop the Butter Tart Ice Cream into bowls or cones and enjoy the rich caramel flavors and buttery goodness reminiscent of traditional butter tarts!

This recipe captures the essence of butter tarts in a creamy frozen dessert, perfect for any occasion. Adjust the amount of pecans and raisins according to your preference for texture and flavor. Enjoy this Canadian-inspired treat that combines sweet and nutty flavors in every bite!

Blueberry Maple Ice Cream

Ingredients:

- 1 cup heavy cream
- 1 cup whole milk
- 1/2 cup granulated sugar
- 4 large egg yolks
- 1 teaspoon vanilla extract
- 1 cup fresh or frozen blueberries
- 1/2 cup pure maple syrup
- Pinch of salt

Instructions:

1. **Prepare the Blueberry Mixture:**
    - In a saucepan, combine the blueberries and maple syrup over medium heat. Cook, stirring occasionally, until the blueberries soften and release their juices (about 5-7 minutes). Remove from heat and let cool slightly.
2. **Prepare the Custard Base:**
    - In a medium saucepan, combine the heavy cream, whole milk, and granulated sugar. Heat over medium heat, stirring occasionally, until the mixture begins to steam. Do not let it boil.
3. **Whisk Egg Yolks:**
    - In a separate bowl, whisk the egg yolks until smooth.
4. **Temper the Eggs:**
    - Gradually pour about half of the hot cream mixture into the egg yolks, whisking constantly to temper the eggs.
5. **Combine and Cook:**
    - Pour the tempered egg mixture back into the saucepan with the remaining cream mixture. Cook over medium heat, stirring constantly with a wooden spoon or spatula, until the mixture thickens and coats the back of the spoon (about 170°F on an instant-read thermometer).
6. **Add Vanilla Extract, Blueberry Mixture, and Salt:**
    - Remove from heat and stir in the vanilla extract. Let the mixture cool slightly.
    - Once cooled slightly, gently fold in the cooled blueberry mixture until it swirls through the ice cream base.
7. **Chill the Mixture:**

- Cover the mixture and refrigerate for at least 4 hours or until completely chilled.
8. **Churn the Ice Cream:**
    - Once chilled, churn the custard base in an ice cream maker according to the manufacturer's instructions until it reaches a soft-serve consistency.
9. **Freeze:**
    - Transfer the churned Blueberry Maple Ice Cream to an airtight container, smoothing the top. Cover and freeze for at least 4 hours or until firm before serving.
10. **Serve:**
    - Scoop the Blueberry Maple Ice Cream into bowls or cones and enjoy the delightful blend of blueberries and maple syrup in a creamy frozen dessert!

This recipe captures the natural sweetness and vibrant color of blueberries, complemented by the rich flavor of maple syrup. Adjust the sweetness of the maple syrup according to your taste preferences for a perfect Blueberry Maple Ice Cream experience.

Tim Hortons Double Double Ice Cream

Ingredients:

- 1 cup heavy cream
- 1 cup whole milk
- 1/2 cup granulated sugar
- 4 large egg yolks
- 1 teaspoon vanilla extract
- 1/2 cup strong brewed coffee, chilled
- 2 tablespoons coffee liqueur (optional, for added flavor)
- Pinch of salt

Instructions:

1. **Prepare the Coffee Mixture:**
   - Brew a strong cup of coffee and let it cool to room temperature. For richer flavor, you can chill the coffee in the refrigerator.
2. **Prepare the Custard Base:**
   - In a medium saucepan, combine the heavy cream, whole milk, and granulated sugar. Heat over medium heat, stirring occasionally, until the mixture begins to steam. Do not let it boil.
3. **Whisk Egg Yolks:**
   - In a separate bowl, whisk the egg yolks until smooth.
4. **Temper the Eggs:**
   - Gradually pour about half of the hot cream mixture into the egg yolks, whisking constantly to temper the eggs.
5. **Combine and Cook:**
   - Pour the tempered egg mixture back into the saucepan with the remaining cream mixture. Cook over medium heat, stirring constantly with a wooden spoon or spatula, until the mixture thickens and coats the back of the spoon (about 170°F on an instant-read thermometer).
6. **Add Vanilla Extract, Coffee, Coffee Liqueur, and Salt:**
   - Remove from heat and stir in the vanilla extract, chilled coffee, coffee liqueur (if using), and a pinch of salt. Mix until well combined.
7. **Chill the Mixture:**
   - Cover the mixture and refrigerate for at least 4 hours or until completely chilled.
8. **Churn the Ice Cream:**

- Once chilled, churn the custard base in an ice cream maker according to the manufacturer's instructions until it reaches a soft-serve consistency.

9. **Freeze:**
   - Transfer the churned Tim Hortons Double Double Ice Cream to an airtight container, smoothing the top. Cover and freeze for at least 4 hours or until firm before serving.

10. **Serve:**
    - Scoop the Tim Hortons Double Double Ice Cream into bowls or cones and enjoy the rich coffee and creamy flavors reminiscent of a classic Canadian coffee order!

This recipe captures the essence of a Tim Hortons Double Double in a cool and creamy dessert. Adjust the amount of coffee or coffee liqueur according to your taste preferences for a perfect Tim Hortons Double Double Ice Cream experience.

Red Velvet Cake Ice Cream

Ingredients:

- 1 cup heavy cream
- 1 cup whole milk
- 1/2 cup granulated sugar
- 4 large egg yolks
- 1 teaspoon vanilla extract
- 1 tablespoon cocoa powder
- 1/2 cup red velvet cake crumbs (from prepared red velvet cake)
- 1/4 cup cream cheese, softened
- Red food coloring (optional, for deeper color)
- Pinch of salt

Instructions:

1. **Prepare the Custard Base:**
    - In a medium saucepan, combine the heavy cream, whole milk, and granulated sugar. Heat over medium heat, stirring occasionally, until the mixture begins to steam. Do not let it boil.
2. **Whisk Egg Yolks:**
    - In a separate bowl, whisk the egg yolks until smooth.
3. **Temper the Eggs:**
    - Gradually pour about half of the hot cream mixture into the egg yolks, whisking constantly to temper the eggs.
4. **Combine and Cook:**
    - Pour the tempered egg mixture back into the saucepan with the remaining cream mixture. Cook over medium heat, stirring constantly with a wooden spoon or spatula, until the mixture thickens and coats the back of the spoon (about 170°F on an instant-read thermometer).
5. **Add Vanilla Extract, Cocoa Powder, and Salt:**
    - Remove from heat and stir in the vanilla extract, cocoa powder, and a pinch of salt. Mix until well combined.
6. **Prepare the Red Velvet Cake Crumbs:**
    - Crumble the red velvet cake into small crumbs. You can use leftover cake or bake a small batch specifically for this purpose.
7. **Add Cake Crumbs and Cream Cheese:**
    - In a bowl, mix the softened cream cheese until smooth. Gradually add the custard base mixture, mixing well to incorporate.

- Gently fold in the red velvet cake crumbs until evenly distributed throughout the ice cream base. If desired, add a few drops of red food coloring for a deeper red color.
8. **Chill the Mixture:**
    - Cover the mixture and refrigerate for at least 4 hours or until completely chilled.
9. **Churn the Ice Cream:**
    - Once chilled, churn the custard base in an ice cream maker according to the manufacturer's instructions until it reaches a soft-serve consistency.
10. **Freeze:**
    - Transfer the churned Red Velvet Cake Ice Cream to an airtight container, smoothing the top. Cover and freeze for at least 4 hours or until firm before serving.
11. **Serve:**
    - Scoop the Red Velvet Cake Ice Cream into bowls or cones and enjoy the rich flavors and creamy texture reminiscent of red velvet cake!

This recipe captures the decadent flavors of red velvet cake in a cool and creamy dessert. Adjust the amount of cake crumbs and red food coloring according to your preference for texture and color. Enjoy this Red Velvet Cake Ice Cream as a delightful treat for any occasion!

Maple Walnut Crunch Ice Cream

Ingredients:

- 1 cup heavy cream
- 1 cup whole milk
- 1/2 cup maple syrup
- 1/2 cup chopped walnuts, toasted
- 4 large egg yolks
- 1 teaspoon vanilla extract
- Pinch of salt

Instructions:

1. **Prepare the Custard Base:**
    - In a medium saucepan, combine the heavy cream, whole milk, and maple syrup. Heat over medium heat, stirring occasionally, until the mixture begins to steam. Do not let it boil.
2. **Toast the Walnuts:**
    - In a dry skillet over medium heat, toast the chopped walnuts until they are lightly browned and fragrant, stirring frequently to prevent burning. Remove from heat and let cool.
3. **Whisk Egg Yolks:**
    - In a separate bowl, whisk the egg yolks until smooth.
4. **Temper the Eggs:**
    - Gradually pour about half of the hot cream mixture into the egg yolks, whisking constantly to temper the eggs.
5. **Combine and Cook:**
    - Pour the tempered egg mixture back into the saucepan with the remaining cream mixture. Cook over medium heat, stirring constantly with a wooden spoon or spatula, until the mixture thickens and coats the back of the spoon (about 170°F on an instant-read thermometer).
6. **Add Vanilla Extract and Salt:**
    - Remove from heat and stir in the vanilla extract and a pinch of salt. Mix until well combined.
7. **Chill the Mixture:**
    - Cover the mixture and refrigerate for at least 4 hours or until completely chilled.
8. **Churn the Ice Cream:**

- Once chilled, churn the custard base in an ice cream maker according to the manufacturer's instructions until it reaches a soft-serve consistency.

9. **Add Toasted Walnuts:**
    - During the last few minutes of churning, add the toasted chopped walnuts to the ice cream maker, allowing them to mix evenly into the ice cream.
10. **Freeze:**
    - Transfer the churned Maple Walnut Crunch Ice Cream to an airtight container, smoothing the top. Cover and freeze for at least 4 hours or until firm before serving.
11. **Serve:**
    - Scoop the Maple Walnut Crunch Ice Cream into bowls or cones and enjoy the creamy maple flavor with crunchy toasted walnuts in every bite!

This recipe captures the delicious combination of maple syrup sweetness and crunchy walnuts, perfect for a refreshing dessert. Adjust the amount of maple syrup and walnuts according to your taste preferences for a perfect Maple Walnut Crunch Ice Cream experience.

Saskatoon Berry Swirl Ice Cream

Ingredients:

- 1 cup heavy cream
- 1 cup whole milk
- 1/2 cup granulated sugar
- 4 large egg yolks
- 1 teaspoon vanilla extract
- 1 cup fresh or frozen Saskatoon berries
- 1/4 cup Saskatoon berry jam or preserves
- Pinch of salt

Instructions:

1. **Prepare the Saskatoon Berry Mixture:**
   - In a saucepan, combine the Saskatoon berries and Saskatoon berry jam (or preserves) over medium heat. Cook, stirring occasionally, until the berries soften and release their juices (about 5-7 minutes). Remove from heat and let cool slightly.
2. **Prepare the Custard Base:**
   - In a medium saucepan, combine the heavy cream, whole milk, and granulated sugar. Heat over medium heat, stirring occasionally, until the mixture begins to steam. Do not let it boil.
3. **Whisk Egg Yolks:**
   - In a separate bowl, whisk the egg yolks until smooth.
4. **Temper the Eggs:**
   - Gradually pour about half of the hot cream mixture into the egg yolks, whisking constantly to temper the eggs.
5. **Combine and Cook:**
   - Pour the tempered egg mixture back into the saucepan with the remaining cream mixture. Cook over medium heat, stirring constantly with a wooden spoon or spatula, until the mixture thickens and coats the back of the spoon (about 170°F on an instant-read thermometer).
6. **Add Vanilla Extract and Salt:**
   - Remove from heat and stir in the vanilla extract and a pinch of salt. Mix until well combined.
7. **Swirl in the Saskatoon Berry Mixture:**

- Once cooled slightly, gently fold in the cooled Saskatoon berry mixture until it swirls through the ice cream base. Avoid mixing too thoroughly to maintain the swirl effect.

8. **Chill the Mixture:**
   - Cover the mixture and refrigerate for at least 4 hours or until completely chilled.
9. **Churn the Ice Cream:**
   - Once chilled, churn the custard base in an ice cream maker according to the manufacturer's instructions until it reaches a soft-serve consistency.
10. **Freeze:**
    - Transfer the churned Saskatoon Berry Swirl Ice Cream to an airtight container, smoothing the top. Cover and freeze for at least 4 hours or until firm before serving.
11. **Serve:**
    - Scoop the Saskatoon Berry Swirl Ice Cream into bowls or cones and enjoy the refreshing blend of Saskatoon berries and creamy ice cream with delightful swirls throughout!

This recipe captures the unique flavor of Saskatoon berries in a creamy frozen dessert, perfect for enjoying the flavors of the Canadian prairies. Adjust the sweetness of the Saskatoon berry mixture according to your taste preferences for a perfect Saskatoon Berry Swirl Ice Cream experience.

Maple Bacon Pecan Ice Cream

Ingredients:

- 1 cup heavy cream
- 1 cup whole milk
- 1/2 cup maple syrup
- 4 slices of bacon
- 1/2 cup chopped pecans, toasted
- 4 large egg yolks
- 1 teaspoon vanilla extract
- Pinch of salt

Instructions:

1. **Prepare the Bacon:**
   - Cook the bacon slices until crispy in a skillet over medium heat. Once cooked, drain on paper towels to remove excess grease. Let cool and chop into small pieces.
2. **Prepare the Custard Base:**
   - In a medium saucepan, combine the heavy cream, whole milk, and maple syrup. Heat over medium heat, stirring occasionally, until the mixture begins to steam. Do not let it boil.
3. **Whisk Egg Yolks:**
   - In a separate bowl, whisk the egg yolks until smooth.
4. **Temper the Eggs:**
   - Gradually pour about half of the hot cream mixture into the egg yolks, whisking constantly to temper the eggs.
5. **Combine and Cook:**
   - Pour the tempered egg mixture back into the saucepan with the remaining cream mixture. Cook over medium heat, stirring constantly with a wooden spoon or spatula, until the mixture thickens and coats the back of the spoon (about 170°F on an instant-read thermometer).
6. **Add Vanilla Extract, Chopped Bacon, Chopped Pecans, and Salt:**
   - Remove from heat and stir in the vanilla extract, chopped bacon pieces, toasted chopped pecans, and a pinch of salt. Mix until well combined.
7. **Chill the Mixture:**
   - Cover the mixture and refrigerate for at least 4 hours or until completely chilled.
8. **Churn the Ice Cream:**

- Once chilled, churn the custard base in an ice cream maker according to the manufacturer's instructions until it reaches a soft-serve consistency.

9. **Freeze:**
   - Transfer the churned Maple Bacon Pecan Ice Cream to an airtight container, smoothing the top. Cover and freeze for at least 4 hours or until firm before serving.

10. **Serve:**
    - Scoop the Maple Bacon Pecan Ice Cream into bowls or cones and enjoy the sweet and savory flavors of maple syrup, bacon, and crunchy pecans in every bite!

This recipe captures the unique combination of maple syrup sweetness, smoky bacon flavor, and crunchy pecans in a creamy frozen dessert. Adjust the amount of maple syrup, bacon, and pecans according to your taste preferences for a perfect Maple Bacon Pecan Ice Cream experience.

www.ingramcontent.com/pod-product-compliance
Lightning Source LLC
LaVergne TN
LVHW081556060526
838201LV00054B/1923